To all the souls I've met and will meet during my lifetime and to all who are still looking to find joy and purpose in their lives.

One Life To Be You

An inner self journey to reinvent your job, your corporate career and your life

Juliana Tabares

One Life To Be You

Copyright

All rights reserved. No part of this book may be reproduced in any form without permission in writing from the author. Reviewers may quote brief passages in reviews.
Pereira, Risaralda, Colombia
1st edition published in 2018
2nd edition published 2023
Copyright © Juliana Tabares, 2023

Disclaimer

No part of this publication may be reproduced or transmitted in any form or by any means, mechanical or electronic, including photocopying or recording, by any information storage and retrieval system, or by email without the author's written permission.

Neither the author nor the publisher assumes any responsibility for errors, omissions, or contrary interpretations of the subject matter. Any perceived slight of any individual or organization is purely unintentional.

Brand and product names are trademarks or registered trademarks of their respective owners.
Cover Design: Juliana Tabares
Editing: Daniel Johnson and Steve Patterson

Table of Contents

Introduction 7
Chapter 1 – A Comfort Zone Full of Discomfort 11
Chapter 2 – A Constant Dissatisfaction 25
Chapter 3 – It's Never Too Late for a Change 41
Chapter 4 – You Are a Product of Your History and Your Surroundings 51
Chapter 5 – Understanding Your Human Nature and Your Values 71
Chapter 6 – Measuring Equilibrium 99
Chapter 7 – Defining Real Success 143
Chapter 8 – Trust Yourself 157
Chapter 9 – Purpose and Passion 201
Chapter 10 – Plan Your Life 217
Chapter 11 – The Best Version of You 237
Chapter 12 – Creating New Habits 263
Chapter 13 – Plan Your New Career 295
Chapter 14 – Just Do It 319
Acknowledgments 339
About the Author 341
Thank You 343

Introduction

I had reached a breaking point when I decided to quit my job. I was tired of waking up unmotivated to go to work every day only to see people complaining in their corporate jobs, apart from their families, putting their health at risk and feeling discouraged. I couldn't help but wonder if all we get to do is spend the best moments of our lives working for a big corporation or a firm whose vision and values are far from what we should be doing. Was life only about this?

I started searching desperately for a purpose, a passion, a reason to be alive. I thought for some time that saving the environment was my mission. I was so hopeless that I forced myself to believe in that. With time, through reading and coaching, I discovered that what I needed to change was not the external world but my own. The way I embraced life, the way I understood it.

Only when one of my mentors told me I would find my purpose in the things that hurt me the most did I realize what it was. It took me a while to understand, but I can visualize it today. The answer I found was likely always with me. Sometimes what you seek may be seen as evident when you discover it, as if it was right before you your whole life. Both my purpose and passion are illustrated in this book in every word, phrase, and paragraph.

Today, I'm in front of a computer writing the introduction of a book I dreamed of as far back as I can remember. I never knew what I would write about, but now I know that every time I said out loud, "I want to write a book," I was paving the path to this moment. This book, written in this particular time and place, will help people like me who feel trapped in a job that makes them miserable. We are so blinded by our programs and fears that we cannot see all the world's opportunities. We are too plugged into "the systems" that we don't have time to stop and think about what we are doing here, in this world. It may sound existential, but discovering our true purpose and calling, can be the most important duty to fulfill in our lifetime. So far, we only know this form of life; and as we don't know what will happen after we die, we shouldn't be wasting the only opportunity we are confident we have.

Whatever the reason is for you to have this book in your hands, I want you to understand one thing; this is not a book to criticize or a book against working for consulting firms or big corporations. ONE LIFE TO BE YOU is a book about how you feel as an individual in the place you decided to spend the majority of your time, the company for which you have decided to work. It's a book to discover why sometimes you feel unhappy, why sometimes you feel unsatisfied, and why sometimes you feel you dislike your job. But overall, this is a book to transform your thoughts and seek the beginning of a beautiful life.

This book is not against people or leaders out there trying to do what is right, like helping firms and their employees achieve their strategies or professional goals. Those leaders at the top of the organizations are doing, as the rest of us, what they believe is proper. This book, however, could be an eye-opener for those starting their careers. It can be a tool for companies to take the first step toward the future of the business world. It can also be a decision-making tool to move to another level of your life. Or just a book that speaks to you for other reasons.

Another objective of this book is for you, the reader, to understand that you are not alone in this competition of life. All humans are made the same and driven by similar fears and dreams. However, regardless of where you are in your career, there is always another way; there is always another way to improve your life to feel happier and fulfilled.

This book is my way of telling you to stop your fear of being yourself. Go out there and scream to the world what you think, what you really believe in, with no hesitation, with love, with pure and total integrity. We only have one life to be ourselves. We have only today to make the best of it. So now is the time to start investing in things that fill your spirit with calm and make you feel joy.

You should take this book and read it as the first investment of time and energy toward finding the life you always wanted. Invest in you and only in you. Never put your partner or your children before you, they are the creators of their own lives, and you should let that go. We won't find happiness through the lives of others or the experiences of others. That is, in fact, a very selfish thought because if you believe that your happiness depends on others, you will be only expecting to receive from them. But if you work on yourself, you will become the best version of you and be ready to give pure and unconditional love without expecting anything from anybody.

...

In chapter one, you will learn why you may feel unhappy in your work and identify yourself with three different types of employees. In chapter two, I will share my personal experience and the process I had to pass through to deeply understand how I would embrace life and move toward the challenges unfolding. In chapter three, I consolidate a personal transformation method and summarize each step to deciding what path you want to take in your professional life. In the remaining chapters, you will explore these steps more deeply, including theories, scientific research, personal growth frameworks, and tools to help you rediscover your authentic self. Let me guide you to one of the best journeys of your life—the journey to find your purpose.

Chapter 1 – A Comfort Zone Full of Discomfort

"Unless you give motivated people something to believe in, something bigger than their job to work toward, they will motivate themselves to find a new job, and you'll be stuck with whoever's left."

- Simon Sinek -

Before writing this book, I interviewed more than 40 people who were working or had worked for consulting, accounting, law firms, and big corporations. They represented all levels of the organization: from starting their career to arriving at the summit as partners and directors. I also interviewed people working in different countries and from different nationalities; your culture and the market you work for influence how you feel about it. But regardless of where you are in your career, which country you are from or what type of firm you work for, the drivers that make you question if is worth working for a company are, in fact, very similar.

In this first chapter, you will discover different concepts that keep most employees of firms and big corporations motivated to go to work every day. Then, you will identify yourself with one of three types of employees according to your mindset toward your job. Finally, at the end of the chapter, you will have the opportunity to recognize why you think you are unhappy and unmotivated.

The Promised Paradise

The promise of long-term and sustained growth in a traditional hierarchy structure or a pyramidal organization is one of the main incentives for joining a firm or a big corporation. Becoming a partner or a director someday and having status or company shares is what I call *The Promised Paradise*. Every year, a little step toward paradise keeps that internal drive on fire. Knowing that in two, three or four years, you'll be in a very different position, with a different job title and a significant increment in your salary, is the main reason most people are motivated to work. Being secure in self-realization is a significant motivator, which also includes the security, comfort and the future of your family.

I call the group, working to become partner or director someday, the *Visionary Followers*. They believe in the system, in the company, and, in many cases, allow the company to be the primary driver of their lives, the cornerstone of their existence.

The promise of having the opportunity to grow is one of the main speeches you hear before joining a company. It is in the DNA of firms, and everything moves around this idea. Most of them have clearly defined the path you need to follow, the map of your professional career. They have defined the goals, the characteristics and the qualities you have to work on to reach the summit into a checklist of requirements for advancing and moving forward in your career. They have followed the best human resources practices, encouraging the definition of a set of skills and competencies to measure people's performance. But even when they develop distinctive and systematic approaches to make this process less subjective, most people feel that this is not the fundamental consideration in allowing an employee to jump from level to level.

In my conversations with former employees of firms and corporations, I found that people who believed their promotion was based on the requirements checklist were those at the beginning of their careers. People who have been in the business for ten or more years believe that the actual game for promotion and success opportunities differs and depends more on the "political" game played within the organization. I won't say that the feedback and review systems don't work; it's a valuable tool to collect, analyze and identify the competencies, skills and goals individuals should possess to deliver a good service. However, I could detect the frustration in their voices when talking about the promotion process. It is hard to comprehend why you still did not make it if you had the perfect checklist and did everything you were told. But sometimes, the reason is that these are businesses, and everything needs to be meticulously planned. Firms cannot start promoting every employee who meets the minimum criteria of the checklist. Companies must ensure sustainability to run their business and support partners or owners. If there is no clear growth projection in the market, you cannot put the stability of the pyramid at risk. Ultimately, the promised paradise won't be for everybody but for very few.

In some other cases, it is not clearly stated that the market conditions are part of the prerequisites for the promotion. This request is not normally disclosed. Rarely will you hear the honest and transparent statement: "this is a business, and not everyone has the same opportunities to grow, even if you meet all the requirements." The leaders cannot do so because that is like a bucket of cold water on the engine that keeps people running to work every morning. I don't know whether the promotion propaganda is being delivered consciously or unconsciously. Still, I believe most people have good hearts and want everybody to grow and do the best for their lives, even when the evidence shows that it is impossible.

The Circle of Trust

Then, there is another reason some people don't reach the top. It is not the checklist or the conditions of the market. The reason is that they don't belong to what I call *The Circle of Trust* or the political game.

The Circle of Trust is not a Machiavellian organization formed by the Knights Templar that possesses the secrets of the partnership. It is not a conspiracy theory created by those who did not make it to the top and are jealous. It is just the result of the pure essence of human behavior.

Unconscious or not, biased or not, we tend to be surrounded by people we trust, who tend to be people with similar backgrounds, ways of thinking, goals and beliefs. You don't want to work with people who could ruin your reputation, project and career. So, like magnets, people with the same level of energy tend to attract to each other, and promotion is the result of this attraction.

It's likely that a company's leaders today are similar to the leaders it had 100 years ago or when it was founded. Little by little, the people who continue growing in the organization form *The Circle of Trust* and carry the same beliefs and expectations that leaders and founders had years ago. The culture and the values spread as the company expanded, rooting in all aspects of an organization: the strategy, the goals, the list of competencies required to be promoted, and the people—especially the ones who make it to the top. However, there are many other explanations for the values of a firm and how this affects your stability and well-being. I will elaborate on this in chapter five.

The Business Relationship

Many employees, and possibly you, sooner or later realized that the dream of being a director or a partner is only for some. Many finally understand that climbing to the top of the pyramid is not a reality. Whatever the situation is, whether it is because the employees believe they are not good enough for the company or the checklist is long and hard to complete. Others may have accepted that they are not part of *The Circle of Trust,* so there is no point in trying to compete. Or, simply, the idea of becoming partners or directors is not appealing to them anymore; they want to pursue something other than the life they see of their partners and directors. I call this group of employees the *Traders of the Real.*

The Promised Paradise, the primary fuel for the engine, doesn't work for this group; they are more rational. They accept working for the firm regardless of the lack of paradise. It's a puzzle to understand what motivates the *Traders of the Real* who stay in a firm that doesn't fit them. It is not a secret that working for a firm or a large consulting corporation is one of the most time-consuming jobs in the world. Whether high season or low season, you need to be ready to start your day at 8 or 9 a.m. without really knowing when you will be free again. Working during the weekend and being plugged in during vacations is typical for some people. The abnormality here is going on vacation for two weeks without checking your emails.

However, the puzzle of the *Traders of the Real* is to resolve by transforming their relationship with the firm becomes a mere business exchange. They give time and knowledge to the firm, and the firm gives back to their money and benefits. The *Traders of the Real* believe that working for a firm or a big corporation is a good deal. Some believe salaries and bonuses are outstanding, particularly in law firms and consulting, so sometimes it's hard to find a job that pays as much. Others, for example, love traveling and the miles and hotel points they make on every trip and are willing to sacrifice their stability and closeness to their families for traveling as a good part of the deal. In other cases, some enjoy what they do; they like the projects, and they like to serve clients. So even when the promise of partnership or being a director is no longer their motivation, they have decided to stay.

The *Traders of the Real* group differs from the *Visionary Followers* because they are unwilling to sacrifice their whole lives for the firm or the client; they know how to put boundaries. This group has the clarity that their jobs are just a means to an end, a circumstantial task that doesn't have to be considered long-term and definitively does not represent a partnership or a directive job title. They understand that working is just one part of their lives and are waiting for the right opportunity to move, whether to another area, other firms or a job in another sector.

Additionally, the *Traders of the Real* are not resigned to staying and waiting for the situation to improve. They understand the business relationship they decided to have with the firm but are continuously looking for other opportunities. They are actively applying for other jobs or thinking about the perfect start-up. Their ambitions are more significant, and they sincerely believe they deserve a better deal.

If you identify with this group, please do not stop reading forward. Even though you have a pragmatic point of view and you have probably reached a point of controlling your stress and balancing your life, there are many things that this book will teach you. Work is not only a means to an end, and life is not only something that happens to us. Don't limit your life to a mere transaction, especially when you spend most of your life in your office, surrounded by people with whom you don't share the same values. You only live once, and nobody can assure you you will have a blast in your next job if you are not having a blast today.

The Trap of Safety

There is a final group of people, which is the group of people who inspired me the most to write this book. If you are holding this book, you may identify with this group. This group is called the *Caged Dreamers*.

Warning! *Be careful if you feel negative emotions reading the following paragraphs. Usually, the truth affects our deepest feelings and feeds insecurities, so observing those feelings is an opportunity for reflection and introspection. If the words impact you negatively, it could mean you are deeply connected with this group.*

This group doesn't believe in the company, they don't believe in the quality of the products, and overall, they don't believe in their leaders. They believe they are trapped, that there is no alternative or the possibility of a life outside the company. They have not accepted the reality of *The Circle of Trust*, so they feel constantly betrayed by their leaders. And finally, they have not accepted that working for the firm is just a mere exchange relationship like that of the *Traders of the Real*.

They live in constant discomfort, monotony and stress. They tend to work more because they believe that whatever is coming next, a promotion or a bonus, will make them feel better. They are trying to prove to others that they can do it, unconsciously covering up the fact that they don't want to be there; they hate it.

Some of them constantly talk about how bad the situation is and blame the supervisors, the client or the projects. They have allowed the company to drain all their energy, sometimes seriously affecting their health and personal lives. They are blinded by their egos, caught within a system that is always wrong for them.

According to this group, unfair and negative feedback is one of the reasons they feel unmotivated. Any feedback about their performance is usually negative or inexistent. They don't feel they are being treated fairly compared to their peers, and the feedback never reflects the amount of work and energy invested. Therefore promotions, compensation, and bonuses are also short. Furthermore, they haven't accepted that the feedback and evaluation systems are frameworks for guidance because they have not assimilated that unconscious bias and the subjectivity of the human being plays the most crucial role in the performance evaluation systems of companies.

Unclear feedback is also a common dissatisfaction trigger, significantly related to *The Circle of Trust*. As the circle of trust is unconsciously created, there is no good way to tell people, "You know what, we don't feel you can be part of our sacred circle." Thus, even when the formal feedback is positive to motivate a valuable employee, they will not be promoted and will never become partners or directors. At this point, the feedback turns into a tangle of words that may sound like this: "We don't know what is going to happen," "We are not sure you are ready," "There are other things you may improve," or "We are not confident about you." Only in the end, when the employee is no longer useful or becomes too costly, does a transparent and open conversation happen, never before. After all, this is business,

People in this group get confused and easily frustrated. All the time, they see people less prepared to make it to the top and are witnesses of the recruitment of newer members of the company to positions above them, even when they were told there was no room for growth.

The *Caged Dreamers* feel like prisoners whose lives belong to the firm. They are sent to travel and constantly obliged to separate from their families or from the possibility of having a stable life. As they work extra hours without the proper compensation, they feel they are sacrificing themselves for an organization that doesn't care about them. As they have not accepted that their job is their choice or that they are doing it as part of a business transaction, they are prisoners of their own reality. It is a reality where they feel treated as a resource to make money for others. It seems a vast contradiction that people, the most critical asset of a company, feel like chess pieces moved according to the needs of others.

Finally, among the *Caged Dreamers*, there is a subgroup, depending on which country they work in and under which conditions, who feel deeply discriminated against. For example, if you are a woman, you may have less probability of making it or finding the same opportunities and salary as men. Let's be honest, how often are more women than men in a boardroom? However, working for a specific corporation is not what is not offering equal opportunities. The problem is broader and involves the collective mindset and the juncture of the history we are living in now. Discrimination against minorities is an issue that will be discussed later in this book.

In conclusion, stress, monotony and constant dissatisfaction are the main drivers of employees in the *Caged Dreamers* group. They reached the point of waiting for life to happen to them. They have a list of excuses to stay where they are instead of taking control of their lives and future. They cling to the belief that big corporations are the ultimate place to work and to demonstrate that they can be someone successful. But the problem with reaching this mindset is that it is tough to see outside their cage, and after months or even years in the same situation, it is impossible to comprehend that there is an outside world full of opportunities.

I can only tell this group that the years are passing by, and the best moments will be wasted if they keep living in this golden cage created by their mind. They don't have to keep living in a comfort zone full of discomfort. Even when companies should work on motivating people and identifying what they need to feel fulfilled and happier in the workspace, the lack of fundamental action cannot stop you from finding happiness. If companies' strategies are not working, you must work for yourself.

Exercise – Your Dislikes

You may not identify with everything even when you can relate to some things I've mentioned here. Nevertheless, you are the only one who can know why you don't feel satisfied or happy with your work. So, to move forward and start benefiting from what is coming next, recognize and write down why your current situation is not ideal—corporative politics, institutional rules, situations and personal stories that make you feel disappointed and discouraged. Your dislikes list can have five to twenty things or many more; it does not matter.

After you have the list, right next to each dislike, write down the emotion that better describes your feelings in each situation. If those emotions are repeated frequently, do not worry; you are just identifying some of your deepest values, or in other words, you are identifying the antagonists of your values.

Here are some examples of dislikes and feelings I gathered after the interviews with employees or former firms' employees.

Dislikes	Feelings
Lack of trust and transparency	Betrayal and uncertainty
Excessive work and continuous traveling	Anger for not having enough time for my family and me
Being reminded of what you are doing wrong	Lack of confidence, low self-esteem
Work without meaning or without adding value.	Disappointment about life, lack of passion

Chapter 2 – A Constant Dissatisfaction

"I must say a word about fear. It is life's only true opponent. Only fear can defeat life. It is a clever, treacherous adversary, how well I know. It has no decency, respects no law or convention, shows no mercy. It goes for your weakest spot, which it finds with unnerving ease. It begins in your mind, always ... so you must fight hard to express it. You must fight hard to shine the light of words upon it. Because if you don't, if your fear becomes a wordless darkness that you avoid, perhaps even manage to forget, you open yourself to further attacks of fear because you never truly fought the opponent who defeated you."

- Yann Martel, Life of Pi -

In this chapter, I will tell the story about how I discovered the process I am sharing with you in the rest of the book, detailing the specific moments and circumstances that caused me to discover that I needed to change how I embraced life. Then, at the end of the chapter, I will share one of the essential ingredients for every step, decision, thought and moves you make.

The Automatic Mode

I still remember the first time I was offered a job as a consultant for one of the biggest firms in the world. I felt very motivated and prideful. My success story had just started, and I was going to build an unprecedented future working for a multinational company. I bet you can still remember your first day like this, all the promises and expectations of growing within a big corporation and someday becoming "someone important."

Over time, the success story vanished into daily activities, deliverables, and deadlines. The optimistic dreamer who first joined the firm disappeared. Instead, I became more worried about what time I could leave the office, how many hours of sleep I would get and the excessive amount of work I would probably have for the weekend. Little by little, I stopped recognizing myself. The fearless, happy, optimistic and rebellious young lady I was in high school, and my university was disappearing.

I got used to the formality of the firm, and everything changed in my life, or at least it was my perception. The way I dressed and the way I spoke transformed rapidly. At some point, I learned how to mimic all the business world's expressions and behaviors. Even when I still had my points of view and shared them when possible and tried to be authentic, there were many other times when I felt I had to hide what I was thinking. It all seemed like I was building the layers of a new face, a mask.

However, two events took place to open my eyes and take me back on the track of a meaningful life. The first was a phrase that one of my best friends from college told me when visiting years after not seeing each other. After spending an entire weekend together, he told me, "You have changed. You are not the same person I met before. It is like something has drained the best you had inside you." I initially felt slightly offended, but I stopped and tried to understand his point. I looked older, was tired, and had put many pounds on my body. I gained much weight through traveling and eating out, and I did not have a minute to work out.

I also realized that I had stopped doing what I loved the most; climbing, painting, writing and playing the guitar were my favorite things to do when I was younger. I had put my hobbies in second place in my priorities, and I resigned because I knew that it would continue the same: commuting more than three hours a day, working until 8 p.m. or 10 p.m. and having meetings and work to complete during the weekend. I could never bring these old hobbies back into my life. Finally, I accepted that I had grown up; I was an adult, a businesswoman and a potential partner who needed to succeed.

The other event was also during a conversation with a friend who worked as an editor for a television show with nothing to do with the business of big consulting corporations. We talked about our jobs, what we had to do at the office, and our typical days.

Early into the conversation, he stopped me and said, "Juliana, don't believe you are better than others because you work for a big corporation. You are not going to change the world from where you are." After that day, we never spoke again. I felt he had offended me and disregarded my dreams. Today, I wish I had him in front of me to tell him how right he was. I had become a snob who believed I was more incredible than the rest because I was an assistant in a firm.

Nevertheless, what stuck with me was his point about changing the world. I started to realize that what I was doing in my job did not have any legacy. On the contrary, my clients were companies I did not believe in, companies whose products polluted the environment, and companies that disrespected their employees, including external consultants like me. I was participating in the vicious cycle of helping the biggest become bigger with no positive impact on the planet. The worst part was that I had forgotten who I was. I left behind all the things I was passionate about for a job, like someone's life reduced to an office, a desktop and a boss. I was neglecting the most valuable thing I would ever have: my own life.

This glimpse of awakening came and went over several months or years... I cannot even remember. I was so blinded by thinking that I had to pay my bills, healthcare, and student loans. I had no other option but to consider this job as the means to an end. I lived many years of my life in automatic mode. And without knowing, little by little, the person I was disappeared. I let my job destroy my soul and my creativity. I was not doing anything for myself. Every minute, hour and moment of my life was devoted to it, to the firm. I had become a *Caged Dreamer.*

Saving the Planet

Only when I finished paying my student loan and did not have that pressure holding me back did I decide it was time to start looking for a way to save the world. After all, I was looking for a job with a legacy. So after almost seven years in the consulting business, I stopped and looked for answers to give something back. I started reading about NGOs and the environment and coaching myself to identify purpose and passion in my life. Finally, I figured out what I wanted in about a year and prepared a detailed plan.

The final goal was to become a sustainable development expert, helping companies develop strategies and programs to tackle the planet's biggest threats: poverty, hunger, pollution, inequality, etc. I also thought it was the perfect moment to move abroad and get a master's degree. At that time, I used to believe that going back to school was the proper thing to do if you wanted to advance in your career. The sensation was extraordinary because now I was looking for a master's with purpose, so for the first time in my life, I started to believe I had found the meaning I was seeking. I was so excited about that plan that I squeezed it into my busy schedule studying English at 5:30 a.m., studying for the GRE (the test needed to apply to a master's in the USA), and researching universities at night. I finally discovered that when you want to do something and believe in something, there is time for it.

It is hard to recognize myself when I go back in time and observe those moments. I did not understand the power that pulled me out of bed at 5 a.m. and kept me running until midnight to finish each of the GRE exercises, I had scheduled in that plan. The Universe also started to manifest in a way I never expected, like the pieces of a puzzle were finding where they fit. One of the things I remember the most was a typical day at the office when an email popped into my inbox out of nowhere. A university in France had sent me an invitation for an interview. I didn't even remember if I had even heard of that University before. They were recruiting students in my hometown, miles away from France. As unbelievable as it sounds, the interviews took place in the building next to my office. I only had to walk 200 feet.

I could not believe this French school had a master's degree called Sustainable Management and Eco-innovation. At that time, the probability of finding a master's focus on what I wanted was very low, or at least during my research. I hadn't been successful in finding something as precise as this. Today, I think the power that pulled me out of my bed to study English at 5 a.m. was the same creative power that put the school with the master's degree I wanted just next to my office.

However, when life-changing decisions come into your life, forces start pulling toward opposite directions. Always remember this. Not for you to have a pessimistic point of you when making decisions, but to always take additional impetus when you decide to change your life.

For example, when sharing the plan with my friends and family, I did not have the support I expected. I especially remember three punctual conversations. First, one of my friends told me, "Juliana, you are from Colombia, you are poor, and you don't have the means to study abroad." Then, a relative said, "You need to be very careful; you are not 20 anymore, and you can only make these moves when you are younger." Finally, one of my supervisors said, "You are throwing away the last six years of your career at the firm; you are moving backward."

At that moment, I freaked out. I let those comments fill me with fear and hesitation. What if they are right? What if I cannot pay my debt? What if I don't find a job as good as this one? What if I'm too old to start over?

It took me several years to understand that every person gives you advice and comments on your life from their fears and nostalgia. The fact that they have different life manuals does not mean one is wrong; we all have different monsters in our minds and very different ideas of what life means. The reason every person believes we are on this planet is different.

After I finished my master's in France, it took me six months to find a job where they paid me three times what I was making before and in less than three years had paid 90% of my student loan. I will never know if I was too old to start over. Still, I'm sure my 90-year-old self will never look back and wish to trade the experience of studying abroad, traveling through Asia and Europe and learning a third language for five more years at a firm that made me unhappy.

The Awakening Trigger

When I finished my master's degree and a graduation project that I felt very proud of, I started working with my brother-in-law in a startup focused on renewable energies. The plan was working as defined years ago, but something inside me was not yet satisfied. A feeling inside me was looking for something else, something more significant. So, I started again looking for a new job and adding a new experience to my life. After several interviews and recruiting processes, I was again offered a position in a consulting firm. However, this time, I believed it was a little bit "different" because it was in a different country, the United States of America. Full of expectations, I packed again and moved internationally for the third time in less than two years.

Filled with dreams, as if it was the first day of my life, I started this new path, a new challenge. Besides my auditing and consulting job, I joined groups and communities related to sustainable development and corporate social responsibility. The topics I felt more excited and inspired about. But in a matter of months, when the automatic mode retook possession of my spirit, I could only think of delivering, performing, charging hours, invoicing, studying and getting certifications.

Unlike my previous job, I had nights and weekends for me. I was very excited about this, even when it sounded so elemental; it was a game changer. Of course, I was still tired and in automatic mode, but at least I had time for exercising and having a social life.

After two years of committed work, the promotion day was finally here. I had all the business case, meaning this, the checklist of requirements to become a manager: the two-million-dollar project delivered, the good relationships with the client and the team, the extracurricular activities to save the planet and the certification. The plan was working, and nothing could go wrong. But this time, the Universe again had a surprise for me, and my mind was unprepared for that.

The promotion never happened, and all the aspects most people working for firms feel frustrated had invaded me. I had dedicated valuable time of my life to this moment, and no one but me could see my efforts and accomplishments. I was blaming specific people for my disgrace. They did not trust me, so I was useless to them. The feedback received needed to be more transparent; nobody had the guts to tell me what was happening. Therefore, I started blaming my ethnicity. I was a minority, a Latin woman in a world full of men. The constant dissatisfaction of doing a meaningless job only for the biggest to become bigger took over me. I let the lack of purpose in my work drain my energy again. I started to lose hope again.

Anger and frustration followed. I was blaming others and life itself for my destiny. But again, life changed my course of action, and just 24 hours after I was told the bad news, I received a text message from a coach I had met a couple of years ago. When I saw that message, I instantly knew this was also a message from the Universe because, for the first time in my life, I had this inexplicable urge to open up and be honest about my thoughts and feelings regarding my job. Even when the message said a simple "How are you doing?" I knew it was the opportunity my soul needed to let out everything crossing my mind. He called me, and we spoke about my situation and life itself for more than an hour. From that moment and for the next two years, he was a key piece of my reinvention. That conversation marked what I call the beginning of my conscious transformational journey. And for the first time, I understood that I needed an impactful emotional trigger to show me the path to awakening into the reality of my professional life and my life in general—a fundamental reason to pull me out of the automatic mode and out of the system.

The Most Important Ingredient

When I followed what others thought impossible and succeeded beyond expectations, I realized that the force that made me follow my dreams, regardless of what others believed, was self-love and mere trust in myself. At that time, it was just an unconscious decision-making process. I just felt that I had to do what would make me happy, even when it sounded crazy to others. Today, self-love and trust in myself are conscious processes that I implement in every moment and decision of my life.

Everyone is internally fragmented, and there are always different versions of who you are. Therefore, one of the important revelations in life is to understand "who" is making the decisions in your life. One is the side ruled by fear, which usually goes from a realistic point of view to a pessimistic perception of life—the pragmatic one that measures every little movement of your life and thinks everything is going wrong. Then, on the other side, there is one ruled by courage and love that goes from realistic to optimistic—the side of yourself that feels more connected to your heart, feelings, and trust in yourself.

This revelation helped me, for example, to understand that all those feelings of anger after I wasn't promoted came from tons of accumulated fear: the fear of failure. I was even embarrassed to share this with my coworkers. How could I tell them I was so mediocre professional that, after several years of waiting for a promotion, I could not make it? I was ashamed because someone my age should be in a much higher position. I felt that I had failed the firm, I had failed my family, had failed myself. So, to cover up my shame and the lack of opportunities by blaming others, the circumstances and how different I was from the rest.

If this sounds familiar, I suggest you pay extra attention and write down one of my favorite mantras: "You are the creator of your life and the final one accountable for it." Not your boss, not your client, not your team, not the circumstances, only you. Only when you are conscious of this (and we will dig very deep into this throughout the book) will you start making decisions from your courageous side so that you are at peace with yourself and the Universe regardless of the outcome. There is no one to blame; there is nothing you can do but encourage yourself to keep trying and never give up on yourself. Never.

On top of that, making decisions from the side of courage releases much negative energy from your heart. And when I say decisions, I'm not necessarily talking about critical decisions like quitting your job or moving to another country. Instead, I'm talking about little decisions such as the words you speak, the thoughts you have, the new habits, the relationship with others and the commitments to yourself.

It's easy to know when you are making decisions from fear or when you are making decisions from courage or love. The fear side is usually accompanied by external factors like blaming others, comparing yourself to others and feeling ashamed. For example, shame can only exist when you compare yourself with others or care about what others think. But, on the other hand, the loving decision-maker comes from you and only you. The part of you that doesn't need anybody's approval or validation. The part of you that trusts and is always kind to yourself and the world. The part of yourself you feel proud of and always know the right thing to do makes you feel joy and happiness.

After the lovely-you starts to rule your life, a magical unfolding of events begins. First, you start to know yourself better and listen to what you want and not what others want. Second, you start to be conscious that everyone on this planet has a single purpose, and sometimes those purposes are not aligned with your own. Third, you start to understand that the world will not change in your lifetime, and every change you will experience needs to come from you. Finally, after working on you, years of permanent discomfort vanish, and you will start to feel alive again, in love with life instead of being afraid of living.

This moment is the starting point of the journey we will embark on in this book. The following chapters are full of stories, tools and exercises, logically organized in a way that makes sense to your mind. All of them are organized in a framework I call the *Matryoshka Method*, which is divided into two sections: One is designed to understand yourself better, and the second is to reinvent yourself. You will start from the surface of your professional life and move towards the deeper levels of your subconscious, answering questions you never asked before. Little by little, you will better understand the real reason for the discomfort in your life and how to overcome the obstacles keeping you away from your dreams. You will start identifying the internal voice of who you are and what you want to become. The tools are also structured so that you will not need years or decades, like me, to discover your truth or risk never discovering what you truly want in your life. It is time to stop living in automatic mode, as most of us have done for many years. Stop being afraid of following your dreams and listen to the light inside you.

Personal Story – A Trapped Dreamer

As of today, I have quit all the jobs I have had; I think a total of four different times, always trying to find what I think is best for me, what I deserve. I still remember the second time I quit. It was my first official job after I graduated from college. I quit because I was offered a better opportunity that would pay almost 50% more. It wasn't much for someone starting a career, but for me, it was like winning the lottery. I did not have to commute three hours per day, only one. I was going to have a prettier office. And the best prize I won for moving was getting a new boss. I changed from having Darth Vader to Obi-wan Kenobi as my mentor (if you are not a *Star Wars* fan, it was like changing from a very mean boss to an admirable leader). Everything was going to be better and, at the same time, challenging and exciting. I always knew I deserved better, and I made better happen.

I still have a bitter taste when remembering one of my coworkers at the company I left. He was one of the most dedicated and intelligent people I've ever met. He did not only follow orders and understand his tasks perfectly, but he was also kind and helpful. But there was a little problem in his thought— he did not believe he deserved better. He probably thought about it, but he was never really convinced. He didn't know from the bottom of his heart that he had merited a better life.

He had been doing that job for five years, but he did never actually love what he did. There was no passion. Additionally, he knew he could have a better paycheck for what hid did, commitment, and responsibility. He was just too afraid to move and look for better opportunities. He never trusted himself enough to seek the life in his dreams. Fourteen years have passed, and today, I know he is at the same job, at the same desk and probably a salary that has only increased with the country´s inflation. Now, the question is, how long will you wait to realize that you can change your life for good? If you consider it, it may take just a couple of months to be in a better position.

Chapter 3 – It's Never Too Late for a Change

"When I was 5 years old, my mother always told me that happiness was the key to life. When I went to school, they asked me what I wanted to be when I grew up. I wrote down 'happy'. They told me I didn't understand the assignment, and I told them they didn't understand life."

-John Lennon-

In this chapter, I will summarize the structure for the rest of the book, so you have a better idea of what to expect. Implementing some of the tools and exercises in this book may take some time, but you can implement other tools immediately. If you trust me and the process, you will start feeling good today regardless of the moment in life and the situation you are going through. It is never too late for a change, especially when you do it from the most important ingredient: love and courage.

The Change is Within You

The worlds of firms and corporations will not be completely turned around in our lifetime, so if you don't learn to accept this reality, you will continue to feel unsatisfied. That does not mean you should be a conformist and not do your best to enjoy every little moment at your job. On the contrary, enjoying your job is probably one of the situations you should be worried so you can fix it. The previous idea means that fighting the system has to be done differently than what you and all of us have done until now. Protesting the companies' injustice, complaining about their leadership and blaming your job as the leading cause of your unhappiness won't solve anything. Instead, it would help if you started fighting from the inside by using unconventional weapons to change your inner reality in search of one of the fundamental purposes in life: happiness. Some of the following, we will the weapons will be covered within this book:

- Better understanding the system and the truth behind the scenes.
- Taking responsibility for your role within the system and with yourself.
- Finding the keys to finding personal joy and inner peace.
- Welcoming the good things to replicate them in your life and the lives of others.

- Learning about yourself from every situation you dislike so you can transform your mind.
- Improving the system every time you can as it was part of your legacy.

When you are unhappy, resignation from what life has offered will transform into a snowball that will destroy everything. Trying the impossible in your only life is your obligation, not exclusively for you but for your loved ones. Stop believing that real happiness and inner peace are impossible or that nothing will ever be complete. Quit accepting that staying in the meaningless job you hate is normal. Those programs come from a culture of servitude and individuals who haven't tried their hardest to improve their lives. Happiness will not suddenly appear and knock on the door; you must do the work and claim it.

It's never too late to choose happiness. Moreover, you can start being happy today and for every second of your life. However, you have long absorbed the idea that happiness is a fairy tale. The culture and your surroundings have unconsciously programmed you to believe life is hard and full of injustice. But life is, in fact, not full of injustice. Life is what it is, and is the only form of life you are sure exists. As such, it's not enough to say thanks for all you have but to profoundly accept everything life has given you. Accepting all the cards life has put in front of you is your first decision when you want to fall in love with life again.

Accepting is a mandatory step for creating the space and having the energy to start building a life where love reigns.

Do you remember the fear side vs. the love side? I know this may still sound like cliché mumbo-jumbo, but I promise you that through this book, you will prove to yourself that you are putting a lot of unnecessary unhappiness in your life. Whatever you think about your work, the stressful commute, the working hours, the unfair boss, and the annoying coworker... are just products of the limiting beliefs created during your life. Very rarely do people tell us that our destiny and life are written by ourselves, that our internal strength takes us to the life of our dreams. At least, I assumed for many years that the secret of happiness was faith or luck. I never imagined that how I embraced life made the difference between a mediocre life and a life of "success."

However, I want to remind you that the current state of your mind is not necessarily unfair or incorrect. It is just how you were raised and taught to live a socially constructed life. A state of mind that is still yours, and you should accept to start loving yourself more and transforming your life. A state of mind that is unique to you and essential for the future you are creating.

Right now, you may not know what is holding you back, why sometimes you feel stuck in life and how you ended up in a job you hate. You may not comprehend what you did wrong, what decision you made inadequately or why life hasn't unfolded as you always dreamed. However, the answer to whatever is missing and why you cannot feel satisfied and complete goes beyond your job. You are probably giving all you have to the corporate world as if what you do is the definition of who you are and what you are meant to be. Nevertheless, your job is only one of the pieces of a gigantic puzzle.

My goal throughout this book is to help you find out the real reasons for the dissatisfaction in your job and life and to discover when and where that dissatisfaction originates. Only there will you be ready to rebuild who you want to become. Few things will be discovered from the external world, meaning outside your mind and heart. Most of the things in this journey come from within yourself, like understanding who you are and your life purpose. The keys for the path of transformation are only found in your inner self.

The Matryoshka Method

The *Matryoshka Method* is a tool kit I designed to help you define what you want to do in your future and start feeling better about your whole life as soon as possible. Thus, you don't need to wait years or be twenty years old to reconsider how you embrace life. The Method consists of twelve key steps that are in two groups. The first group contains six steps designed to dig and find out what you want and who you are, which I call *"Discover Who You Are."* Most of the things you think about your identity are mistaken and have been defined by others. Your belief systems, the way you have been educated, your culture and your religion have been blocking you from your truth, which is only valid for you and is for you to discover. The second group is an opportunity for you to reinvent yourself to navigate your life better. Only when you understand who and what you are will you be ready to rebuild solid pillars for your life.

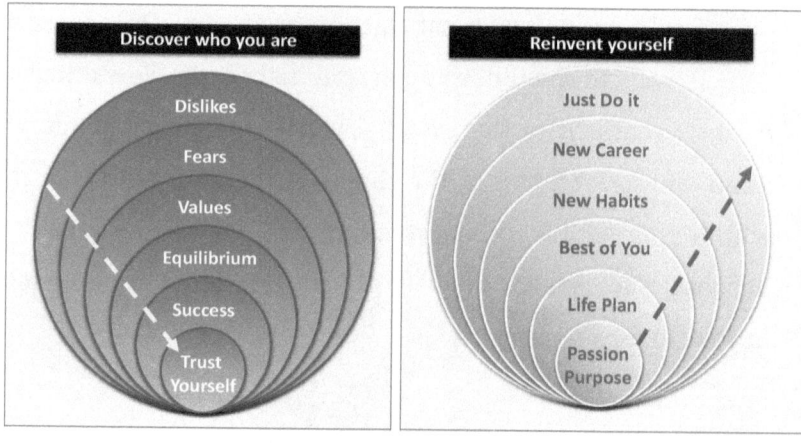

Figure 1- Matryoshka Method Steps

Every chapter of the book is a layer of the *Matryoshka Method*. For example, in chapter one, you will identify your dislikes to understand the real reasons behind the unhappiness at your job and how those manifest in your life. Each layer of the first group represents a more profound step into your subconsciousness, revealing parts of your mind that have been hiding for decades— thoughts, beliefs, ideas, and pain related to your frustration, anxiety or lack of motivation. The last layer of *Discover Who You*

Are ends with the main ingredient of your life, *Trust Yourself.* This crucial stage, the heart of the Method, marks the beginning of defining who you want to become.

All the chapters have one or two exercises, whether a list of thoughts or ideas, a meditation or a mind map. If you want a real, lasting transformation, do not skip the exercises—complete every single one from your heart with the energy you consider worth investing in changing your current situation. You are reprogramming your mind with lighter programs, removing unnecessary loads you are carrying, preventing you from moving forward and resolving what to do with your life.

Buy a journal or a nice notebook. Those pieces of paper can hold the life story you have never told anybody. A story you should put in front of your eyes and heart to reconsider the life you have built and the life you will build. Those pieces of paper will contain the most valuable tools for paving the path for the rest of your life. I am sure you will have fun discovering and writing thoughts you never imagined you had inside or writing changes you never expected to happen in your life. Taking notes of what could be the most important journey of your life, your own story is essential.

Before moving forward, understand that we all deserve and can be happy. It is not exclusively for those born with particular privileges or mere luck. It's for you to decide how to move far from the life that makes you unhappy. And to do so, by the end of the book, you must decide on one of the following three options:

1. Accept, embrace and fall in love again with your current job.
2. Change the situation for a better one where you can start feeling passionate about your job.
3. Leave the situation for good and find a new option.

Staying unhappy is never an option. You only have one life, this one. Yes, I know I already said that a couple of times, but I will repeat it until it is tattooed in your consciousness, and you can see it in all of life's expressions. Knowing that you are wasting the only opportunity to be happy where you spend most of your life may help you act and make a real change. Today is the time to stop wasting your days in remorse.

Consider the cost of living in this situation and what you are sacrificing. Are you sacrificing time with the people you love? have you forgotten about your body and mental health? Are you losing your temper quickly without apparent reason? How much time are you wasting on anxiety, depression, or stress? You are paying a very high price for a very short-term goal: the monthly paycheck. You are causing more harm than wealth to yourself, the people you love, and the universe around you.

Change and finding a job that makes you happy is not a magical recipe or something that will come out from the shadows tomorrow morning. It is a journey inside you from your dislikes, deepest fears and sacred values to discover what your heart truly wants from life. If you don't learn how to listen to yourself and block what the world is telling you to do, it's going to be impossible to find what your soul is looking for, what fills you with passion and excitement. Don't give up on yourself, don't give up on your family, and don't give up on this life. You, like everybody else, deserve to be happy, and as cliché, as it sounds, the answers are only within you. Let's begin.

Personal Story- Uncle Bob

When I started working for the firm, I heard a story that stayed in my mind forever. I never knew if it was true, but it had a meaningful message. One of the sons of a manager in the firm was asked to make a drawing of his family by his kindergarten teacher. When he brought the drawing home, his mom was very proud and looking at the depiction; she said: "Darling, this is beautiful. You and I are in the front, and this is your daddy." The son replied, "No, that's not daddy. That's uncle Bob." The story says that the manager quit the firm the following week.

Something as extreme as this had to happen for him to realize that he was doing something wrong and acting with a lack of integrity. He was neglecting the most valuable treasure in this life. In addition, all the reasons for him to stay at the firm for so long and work so much were based on fear of not having enough to support his family or fear of failure and not being good enough at the firm. However, the cost he ended up paying for keeping that job was more than what he was willing to pay and definitively not more significant than the love for his family.

Chapter 4 – You Are a Product of Your History and Your Surroundings

"You are a slave, Neo. Like everyone else you were born into bondage, born into a prison that you cannot smell or taste or touch. A prison for your mind"

- Lilly and Lana Wachowski, The Matrix -

It is essential to understand your past to understand where you are in your life today. And when I say your past, I'm not only talking about your childhood or where you're coming from as an individual or family member. I'm referring to being a member of civilization and the human race. So, this chapter aims to discover what has shaped who you are by understanding where you come from, your ancestors and the history of our civilization.

Our Place in History

The world has changed enormously, especially after the beginning of the industrial revolution in the late 17th Century—250 years ago. Before that particular moment in England, most of the world consisted of artisans and farmers who mainly worked to meet the basic needs of their families. In many cases, they were also the producers of their foods, clothing, and furniture. Try to imagine a world where having more than two pieces of clothing was a luxury and concepts like cars, leisure trips, and technology were not even part of the vocabulary of the working class.

Only after the first factory opened did employment as we know it today become part of our daily lives. Before that time in history, selling your time was inconceivable for free men. It was the fate that only servants would consider. However, with time and the expansion of cities, employment was a straightforward way to a better life. Hence, farmers started to migrate to the big cities looking for survival, even when employment conditions were not appropriate and, in most cases, deplorable. It was only after the Haymarket Riots in 1886 in Chicago, a century after the industrial revolution, that the workers' movements started to flourish. Thanks to this, the workplace established the eight-hour workday and other benefits such as overtime payments. Before that, what now seems evident in our jobs, like healthcare, paid vacations and bonuses were just unthinkable.

Over 250 years, factories transformed into big corporations and with them, regulations and stock markets. Even when it sounds egocentric, we belong to a particular historical moment. Two hundred fifty years isn't a lot of time. It is only 5% of the known human written history, which started in Mesopotamia around 3000 BCE. This little amount of time, relatively speaking, has documented the most significant technological advances, discoveries, and inventions of our civilization.

Let's do an exercise and try to trace your ancestors over the last 250 years. For example, I can only trace my family for about 150 years, directing to my grandfather's father. Like many people on the American continent, he was born here. Still, only a couple of generations before, our ancestors traveled on ships from Europe to conquer new land, looking for gold for the Queen, religious freedom and escaping from the Black Death. Try to think how far, how many generations, you can trace your ancestors.

Today, without even noticing it, we have coded a little of that history in our brains. Only four generations before, the grandfather of my grandfather was telling him about how the world was in the old continent and advising him about what he had to do to be successful at that time. I imagine something like: "You need to educate yourself, quit farming the countryside and become a successful worker in a big factory." In a different context but with a very similar sentiment, this was the advice given by my grandfather to my mother. Probably, a message not so different from the advice given by your grandparents to you if you were born in the western world. And not far from the advice given by Chinese, Japanese or Nigerian grandparents to their grandchildren. Like if there was a globalized message that has transcended generations and frontiers.

Our parents and we have been the front-row witnesses of the transformation towards a unified world. The stories are becoming more and more universal. With the development of telecommunication and transportation systems, we can effortlessly know how people live on the other side of the world. At the same time, as technological innovations advance, the stories we tell our grandchildren today will be very different from the stories they will tell their own. Artificial intelligence, nanotechnology, biotechnology and genetics will again reshape our meaning of success, as well as the concept of employment we have had since the industrial revolution.

You are the product of the stories said to you; you can't be something different. Your parents are the result of what your grandparents told them, and they are a product of the stories told by their ancestors. Those stories are soaked with everything shaping the culture and the civilization at that precise moment, such as collective fears and the drivers of the status quo.

Even when the stories have change with time, we are all still pursuing something. For example, a thousand years ago, our ancestors were profoundly worried about finding food or a cure for bronchitis and tuberculosis, which were the leading causes of mortality. And today, and thanks to the advances in medicine, we are more worried about getting a better job, traveling, or owning a house, than keeping ourselves alive against infections. The main difference between the past and today, is that today we are not looking for simple survival and we all in search of "the good life."

The Good Life

With the exponential growth of the supply of basic needs for the vast majority of people in the world, the values of our civilization changed. The reasons some societies value and appreciate people today are far from how we valued them before. In a couple of hundreds of years, we passed from being a very poor civilization regarding material things, diseases and daily struggles, to living in a wonderful world full of wealth and abundance. Today people reading this book don't need to worry about what to have for dinner today or about getting a minor surgery to remove their gallbladder. We could say that industrialization, science and technological advances have eliminated many concerns that ruled in the relatively recent past.

If you are between 30 – 60 years old, you will likely be focused on looking for "the good life" for you and your family. In our society, this means having the stereotypical life: make money, buy a house, send your children to college, save for your retirement and get as much entertainment as possible. I'm not saying that this is bad or wrong. I'm just making the point about where we spend most of our energy, as individuals and as an entire civilization. Having the stereotypical life in our world today may be the primary thermometer of having a life with value.

Most working adults today, including you, have "the good life" programs assimilated from the environment your entire life surrounded you.

Since very early in your life, your mind has been absorbing the surroundings you grew up in: the relationships in your family, your kindergarten teacher's stories, your neighborhood atmosphere, your religion's rewards and punishments, your language structure, your culture's traditions and, as we mentioned before, all the ancestral sets of beliefs of your great-great-grandparents. Unconsciously over time, all your experiences solidified into your socially conditioned belief system.

As the noted economist and philosopher Adam Smith may have described it in the 18th Century, it's as if an invisible hand shaped today's world—its development, economy, and markets. Everything has been structured so systematically that it's tough to see outside this system. Trying to understand that there is a different way of living is quite incomprehensible. It is hard, for example, to imagine a society without going to school, getting a job and collecting things. We cannot live outside this world; we all are plugged into this "Matrix."

This invisible hand has rapidly transformed the panorama of our lives, adding new values to our current civilization that unconsciously lead the way we live. Unconsciously because the values you learn from your surroundings were not the reason for you to be sent to school and were never explicitly stated. You captured the idea solely by being born in a specific place and time and under unique circumstances.

Your Unconscious Fears

Every day, similar to the beliefs and values you fight for when going to work to have the "good life," many of your fears are also in a certain way stored in your mind. For some reason, as part of our human nature or how we were raised in the western world, most people tend to act based on fear. As a result, we are more likely to make every little decision in our lives, avoiding something we are afraid to happen instead of looking for what we yearn for.

As an exercise, consider your biggest fear. Don't think about a tragedy or something unlikely to happen, like being attacked by a saber-toothed tiger, kidnapped by space aliens, or dying from a plague. Instead, think as having a brain born in the 20th or 21st Century. Don't try too hard to unlock the fear that defines you; let it come naturally. What is the first thing that came to your mind?

It is natural if nothing self-evident comes to you. Our mind is like an iceberg, so what is on the surface is not necessarily what keeps us awake at night. In other words, most of our worries are deep in our subconscious minds and the less we ask ourselves these questions, the more buried and difficult to observe. For this reason, we will try an additional exercise to start identifying other possible concerns you may not know you have, fears that might be unconsciously driving your life. Let's take a time machine into your mind and travel to your childhood:

- Remember what was the biggest struggle that your parents, grandparents or the person who raised you had?
- Think about your biggest frustrations growing up and the bullying you suffered from your friends and siblings in primary school.
- Consider the child who dreamed about things he/she thought could never get.

Is anything moving deep in your heart? If nothing traumatic comes up or something that can be defined as your biggest fear, don't worry. That only means your fears are still deep at the bottom of the iceberg. Plus, this book is designed to discover and face them by implementing tools and remembering stories that will connect you with answers to questions you have never imagined.

This exercise is essential because the way to face your fears is by moving them from your unconscious to your consciousness, from the bottom to the top of the iceberg. Moreover, you want to understand them because those unconscious fears are the root of your unhappiness and dissatisfaction. And as they are hidden, they make you feel stuck in your life without apparent reason and prevent you from deciding where to start changing your situation.

In addition to unconscious beliefs, we should consider our biology when comprehending the complexity of our minds and recognizing who we are and why we act differently in specific situations. For example, our survival instinct is the most fundamental driver of our human experience, whose primary goal is maintaining ourselves alive. From the moment the modern homo sapiens walked the earth 40,000 years ago to our ancestors 250 years ago and ourselves today, "not to die" is our most critical goal. Every second, our organs, brain and hormones work together to survive so that we can transfer our DNA to the next generation and perpetuate our existence. Therefore, our deepest fears are also related to our human nature and evolution, which we will discuss in more depth in chapter five.

Minorities, Inequality and Discrimination

If you are not a minority because your family was likely never considered poor or discriminated against, you may not personally identify with any of the words in this subtitle. You may only know those terms as the terminology used around social issues that need a solution. However, these concepts and their evolution in our civilization are essential to consider as part of our unconscious beliefs. Not to judge the evolution of our civilization or to feel victims but to understand them as a result of independent events that happened ages ago and collapsed together in our present reality, shaping how we think and live in this modern age.

I want to talk about this topic at this very moment because there may be other fears or beliefs you may need to consider. It is imperative to accept that the invisible hand has penetrated your unconscious mind from the caveman and the Mesopotamian civilization, the industrial revolution, to the current civilization. If you are a minority—for example, a black woman living in the United States—and you are on your way to becoming a director of a big corporation, you and your family probably had to break the 100-year-old program of your beliefs. Someone in your family or yourself had the courage and the spirit to break ground on history and change the destiny of the next generation. It probably was a thought incepted by a single event, situation or person that gave you the necessary courage to transform the history of your future descendants.

However, others with a similar background as your family never overcame those mental programs, thus keeping them in the shadows of an inaccurate narrative. They never believed they could do something extraordinary and therefore did not have the spirit to take the necessary action to effect a change and move forward. They probably lived their entire lives in the neighborhood they were raised and never went to school, making escaping poverty impossible. For them, there is no other life outside the four streets they grew up in—outside the paradigms of their mind.

I'm not saying that discrimination does not exist or that a black woman in a predominantly white business world does not have a more challenging time being successful. My point here is that the difference between the women who succeeded and those who never went to school may be a mere thought, an idea, or a belief that enormously changed how she embraced life for good. I can guarantee it was a conscious choice coming from thoughts such as "I can do it," "I can go to school," "I can be a professional," "I can become a director," and "I will escape this paradigm forever," followed by massively acting to construct a better life.

If our ancestors had difficulty supplying the minimum needs for a decent life, their conditions were much different than today. We were born in a new world that features inequality as a significant challenge. Some had the luxury of being born in what economists call developed countries—where most people can easily supply all their basic needs. Education, health and employment are almost certain for most of the population in countries like Scandinavian Countries, Western Europe, Canada, and Australia.

Others born in developing, undeveloped or third-world countries must struggle more to access supplies of basic needs. In addition, since they were kids, they have learned from teachers, television or the internet that they were born in an unprivileged place compared to others. Therefore, they start to realize they are part of the world's poorest and probably won't get the best opportunities for education and employment. And even when nobody tells them to their faces that they are not good enough for the world, human minds can easily reach such a judgment.

People born and raised in developing countries have a program of inferiority in their minds. If you say to yourself, "I was born in India, but this is not my case," it is probably time to reconsider that thought. For this phase of your life, it is essential to start understanding the reality of your subconscious mind to accept change with courage, acknowledging that the program of inferiority is imperative to move it from your unconscious to your conscious mind. Consciously understanding that you are not less than anybody else is essential to eliminate the beliefs that sabotage you from the life you always wanted.

If born in Switzerland, you would likely run the program of superiority in your mind. You have always known that people go to your country looking for work opportunities and a dignified life. This idea does not suggest you are the cause of the problem or that you are xenophobic or racist; like the rest of us, you have a mindset, unconscious program and beliefs shaped by your surroundings, childhood, and ancestors' history.

Only when you leave your neighborhood, city, country, and continent do you realize that the world doesn't look literally as the economic data depicts. Yes, the data is probably accurate, but when you better understand the reality of the so-called developed countries, you realize that not all that glitters is gold. Or when you go to a less developed country, you also realize that not everything is misery or poverty.

The more awareness you have about the world, the more you start changing your mentality, ceasing the need to feel less or more than anybody and learning that the only real difference between someone being born in a foreign country is their mental programs. In other words, the world created in the minds represents an alien reality. Still, as many still believe, these differences should not be associated with people's mental capacities, creative potential, natural abilities for invention, and moral tendencies.

Regardless of where you were born and the differences in our mentality, fears can be similar in concept because we all are driven by survival instincts, as mentioned before, and programmed by an almost globalized world. What differs from one mindset to another's, is the level of intensity of specific fears.

Think about a person who has a third-world mindset or comes from a low-income family. For them, life is hard, jobs are limited, and money scarcity is that person's biggest fear. Therefore, the likelihood of that person quitting his or her job and looking for better opportunities is less than a person born in a developed country or a wealthy family.

If you grew up in a home that did not have enough resources, you might have a problematic relationship with money. If you grew up with divorced parents, you might have a problematic relationship as a couple. If you grew up with an alcoholic family member, you might have a problematic relationship with alcohol. If you grew up within a religion that said sex is sinful, you might have a problematic relationship with sex. I said, "might have problematic relationships" because reactions from childhood limiting beliefs could also have the opposite impact and unfold positively. Nevertheless, the different aspects of your life have way more chances of being positive if you are aware and conscious of the root of the problem.

As discussed in the previous sections, fears are defined by religion, culture, and the family you were raised. And even when this sounds obvious, you may have never thought about it. You may believe your life is very different from that of your parents or your childhood neighborhood and that you grew up separate from them, but this is mistaken. Your mind is filled with the programs externally imposed from when you were a kid, and only when you interiorize the root of those thoughts and the fears unfolding because of them will you have the power to defeat them. Only then will you realize your life is filled with unnecessary fear and suffering, and you can see your heart's courage and act upon the changes toward the life you want.

Personal Story - A Non-existent France

I have a simple story about how differently we react to the same situations and how this usually is deep in our minds. Understanding this is important to know yourself, identify your unknown fears and be compassionate with the people around you.

A few years ago, I was in a park in a small town in the north of France. The park was full of children and parents on the playground. It was summertime, and the day could not have been more beautiful. Then, suddenly, out of nowhere, an explosion was heard. I guess as this was before the recent terrorist attack had taken place, nobody reacted to the noise. They didn't even move or turn their heads to see where the noise originated.

In my case and a blink of an eye, I jumped, crawled under a bench, and put my hands in over my head. After a few seconds, my mind realized the sound was not an explosion but the backfire of a truck being unloaded next to the grocery store. Just imagine how people must have looked at me. They had no idea what was happing to me. Some could have assumed that I had a mental problem, not even connecting the sound of a truck with my reaction.

My reaction was the result of growing up in the middle of the drug cartel war in Colombia, where bombs and shootings were part of our daily news. Instead, they grew up in a small, tranquil town in France, where bombs are shootings were in movies fiction.

We can only fear what we have seen, told or experienced. And most of our reactions to those fears are, like my reaction — unconscious. And this is true in both cases, simple moments like the story of a non-existent France and significant decisions and events in life.

Exercise – Identifying Your Fears

Before you move forward with your life and make any transcendental decision, it is essential to identify the fears that may be driving your life, and you will do it using a trick.

List all the things you do to escape from reality, purposeless activities to clear your mind when you feel overwhelmed or just as part of your routine. List everything—things that seem harmless such as watching a movie, buying things you don't need, reading a book, or harmful things like smoking, or eating tons of sugar and fast food.

For a week, observe the triggers and the moments where you feel like escaping from the boredom of your work and life and identify what you are trying to escape from or avoid.

- Are you escaping from a conversation?
- Are you escaping from your responsibilities?
- Are you avoiding sharing time with someone?
-Are you avoiding a certain feeling?

- Are you procrastinating something?

These moments tell you a lot about yourself because what you unconsciously avoid is directly linked to fear; thus, for every escapism, identify a fear. Make sure you do this exercise without overthinking or reasoning; your intuition is wiser than your thoughts, which usually take you away from reality. Finally, try to link that fear with the mindset or beliefs of your family, friends, culture and religion. Those mindsets don't have to be clear as water or specific, but simple situations and mere life experiences.

Escapisms, for you to understand me better, don't have a genuine intention or purpose. It is not always about resting after a tough day, doing something you are passionate about or having peace of mind. It is often about unplugging your mind from your life and avoiding the reality you are living.

Social media, for example, is a current form of escapism. For instance, scrolling through what is happening on your Facebook, Instagram or TikTok every five minutes, even when you are at work or having dinner with someone, may reveal something about you and your interaction with reality.

While at work, I used to jump onto social media as a sign of how unhappy I was with it. None of the things I was doing during the day had meaning to me; I felt that I was wasting my life on something that was not important to me or anybody else. My deepest fear was not doing something impactful or not having a voice for transformation. When I link that fear with how I grew up, it can be related to a woman from a developing country, the youngest of two sisters, with the fear of being insignificant and invisible. This fear defines me and drives my need to do something meaningful with my life.

Here is an example of how the chart may look like:

Escapism	Fear	Link with life
Social Media	Not doing something impactful and not having a significant voice	Lack of visibility, unimportant person while growing up

This exercise doesn't have to be perfect, don't worry if you haven't identified your escapisms and fears and how they are connected with your personal life. As I said before, try the exercise without pressure, and work with the first idea that comes to mind. Little by little, as we advance in this book, your mind will start becoming as clear as water. So clear that you won't be disturbed by them anymore.

Moment of Reflection: *Think about your own story and all the events that happened for you to be where you are now. What happened two years ago, 20 years ago, 200 years ago, so you can be here reading this book, in this very room, at this very moment?*

If you don't know what happened 200 years ago, ask your parents and family members how your grandparents lived, what they did for a living, and when they got married, if they did. Also, ask them to tell you stories about the grandfather of your grandfather, where he was born and how he ended up living in the town he died.

Think about the probability of your parents' meeting, and multiply that probability by the encounter of each of your previous ancestors. Aren't we and our lives just the product of a miracle?

Chapter 5 – Understanding Your Human Nature and Your Values

"Every aspect of Nature reveals a deep mystery and touches our sense of wonder and awe.... those with the courage to explore the weave and structure of the Cosmos, even where it differs profoundly from their wishes and prejudices, will penetrate its deepest mysteries."

- Carl Sagan, Cosmos -

So far, we have worked in two of the layers of the *Matryoshka Method*. In chapter one, we identified some of the reasons you may dislike your job, for example, the lack of certainty in becoming a partner or director, unclear or negative feedback, not belonging to the circle of trust, excessive work and never-ending trips, etc. In chapter four, you started identifying the fears you didn't even know you had and how your history and everyday surroundings have grounded those fears. In this chapter, we will focus on our human nature and how this may be linked to some reasons you feel unsatisfied with your job. In the end, and after a general understanding of how our biology may affect our reactions, you will know essential tools to identify your life's most essential compass: your values.

The Human Nature Motivators

Simon Sinek, the well-known optimist, speaker, and writer, explains in his book *Why Leaders Eat Last* the physiological motives of our social behavior. In the book, he describes how the hormones, known as the happiness hormones and the cortisol, affect your daily moods, making you stressed, anxious, and even sick in the workplace. First, I will summarize some of his research and ideas. Then we will dig deeper to discover the motivators and values implicit in our human nature relevant to understanding when passing through an emotional and transitional situation.

…

***Endorphins*:** Endorphins are neurotransmitters related to the runners' high, a pleasurable sensation that today is probably understood better by those participating in marathons. However, hundreds of thousands of years ago, cavemen needed endorphins to have the motivation to go hunting and find the food supply for the day. It was a survival mechanism that motivated the hunter and made their body feel less pain and have fewer adverse effects from stress. This perfect evolution of our nervous system allowed the survival of our species.

Dopamine: Dopamine is a neurotransmitter associated with satisfaction and pleasure. It is also known as the goal-oriented hormone because it is related to the feeling of achieving something. It works like the reward system of human evolution. Unfortunately, this hormone is also associated with addictions—social media, gambling, and alcohol.

Serotonin: Serotonin, another neurotransmitter, is the selfless hormone. The hormone of leadership and approving feelings. As Simon says, this hormone is the one that marks the relationship with our leaders or our teachers.

Oxytocin: Oxytocin is the social hormone, the hormone of love, trust, and empathy. Essential not only to sustain romantic relationships but also to the existing links between parents and children. It is directly related to the powerful survival instincts we spoke of in our previous chapter.

The last one is the hormone Simon called "the Big C"—*cortisol*: the stress hormone. This hormone prepares our body for fighting or flying when we feel threatened.

...

This mixture of hormones and your lifetime unconscious beliefs are responsible for your automatic reactions and continuously controlling your moods and emotions. Knowing this is important because when you are aware of your chemical reactions triggered by situations and experiences, dealing with them becomes less empiric and more controllable. Your most primitive emotions may be controlled by millions of years of evolution, but when you learn to control your mind, you become more assertive in many situations. To better understand which chemicals, hormones, or neurotransmitters are ruling your work life I want to share some concepts for your introspection.

Endorphins have two reactions in the system: the first is to have pleasurable feelings, and the second is to relieve the pain when you have an injury. If you often exercise, you might be familiar with your feelings the day you train or run 5k at 6 a.m. versus the sensations when you don't work out at all. However, endorphins are not only released when you exercise; they also can be naturally boosted when you receive a massage, have sex, dance to a song and meditate. When the level of endorphins is stable, you will feel content during the day. They will help you feel good when you are in a hurry, jump out of bed, and run to the metro station. They also provide the extra energy needed to stay at the office until midnight.

On the contrary, when your level of endorphins is deficient, it may increase the negative perception of your days. Therefore, ruing to the metro station or staying at the office would be less comfortable. This situation will also increase your pain if you suffer from any condition or aggravate the muscular pain due to the ever-lasting work on your desk. Ultimately, a deficiency in endorphin levels will exacerbate your stress and anxiety.

Dopamine keeps you motivated and focused toward a big goal—a project you are eager to see completed —by providing a pleasurable sensation. If the work you are doing is motivating and challenging, if you are implementing a new innovative system, or if you are the manager of an influential transaction, dopamine might positively influence your days. The thirst to see this project implemented and the idea of reaching the pinnacle of your career may be the primary stimulant for dopamine.

When your job is just the means to an end, meaning you are a *Trader of the Real,* dopamine can keep your motivation elevated even when it does not come from the office but from a side gig, business idea or hobby. You know that whatever job you have today is momentary, and your real motivation is ruled by that parallel objective or a plan B.

In addition to a big goal and the dream of completing a meaningful project, dopamine is released in your body every time you complete a specific task. Dopamine is continuously released if you work in an environment that allows completing tasks and closing significant activities. Instead, working for a stagnant company where activities are hard to complete, and projects never conclude, dopamine levels may run low among its employees. This lack of dopamine may create a sensation of frustration and lack of motivation rather than pleasure and focus.

Since dopamine has also been studied to be addictive, it is necessary to consider that there is an immense difference between naturally segregating dopamine and artificially through substances and unhealthy habits. When you do pleasurable things like eating sugar, fast food, recreational drugs, smoking and drinking, the brain releases dopamine to the body generating an additional pleasurable sensation. This knowledge revealed that addictions are not only related to the substance consumed but the dopamine and the sensation this produce in your body.

Therefore, when people do not get the natural dopamine levels needed to operate normally, they unconsciously compensate for the void with external stimulation, for example, substance abuse that harms the body and other escapisms that seem less harmful, like gambling, video games and social media, but that can also have catastrophic consequences for the body and the mind. Moreover, when dopamine levels go the other direction and over increase, the reaction in the body is also unbeneficial. It can affect the sleep cycles and boost your impulses and aggressivity.

Serotonin is the hormone related to pride, admiration, and a sense of purpose. It is connected to the excitement you feel every time you arrive at your office or your client's office and interact with a team that admires you and finds inspiration in you. The energy and enthusiasm experienced as a result of belonging to something bigger than yourself is a direct result of serotonin. This hormone rules the *Visionary Followers* that want to make partners or directors someday, as we saw in the book's first chapters.

Similarly, the admiration of a leader also activates this hormone. And when I say leader, I am not only referring to a leader within a corporate organization. Political or religious leaders can also trigger the release of this hormone; admiration and a sense of belonging are also activated in such bonds.

The previous point is critical in a world that has lost credibility in God and governments—unconsciously transferring the need for belonging to a religion or political party toward the workplace. This reality adds an immense responsibility to the leaders in firms and corporations. When leaders are mediocre, don't have a clear purpose, lack empathy and cannot inspire others, their teams and themselves will likely feel down and tense in the work environment. This can be directly related to the scientific research that has conclude that low serotonin levels are linked to depression. However, after decades of acknowledging this relation, the true origin of depression is still controversial. Which came first: the chicken or the egg?

Finally consider, for your personal life, that serotonin production is not limited to the relationship with our leaders but is also naturally boosted by sunlight, exercise, diets rich in specific proteins and minerals, and probiotics.

The final happiness hormones, oxytocin, is the hormone of trust, love and empathy. Even when it has other vital functions during childbirth and breastfeeding and is also present in men for the production and transportation of testosterone, oxytocin plays an essential role in our moods. This hormone, likewise endorphins, is also boosted during exercise or sex or when we do activities as a group, like singing to music.

This hormone is also stimulated when team members trust each other, and their leader is approachable. On the contrary, when leadership is distant, and there is no camaraderie among team members, distrust sets the tone of the work environment. In such conditions, commitment and engagement are challenging to achieve. Therefore, it directly affects the performance and results within the companies. These assertions are also supported by the late understanding of Darwin's Theory of evolution, which promotes that the survival of the fittest was not only key to the development of our species but empathy and connection within the communities.

In addition, low levels of oxytocin, likewise serotonin, are linked to certain types of depression. Even when people could counterbalance the effects of a hostile environment with the oxytocin they release in their personal life, around their children and spouse, this is not accessible for everybody. Unfortunately, since we live in a world with more single-person households every day, it is expected that most "love" we need for a balanced life must come from the work environment.

If you don't feel safe, motivated, and inspired around the people you spend most of your life with or the leaders you work for, you will affect your happiness hormones' balance and open the door for stress, and with it to the Big-C. The cortisol is likely more frequent among the *Caged Dreamer* group's minds, bodies and moods. This situation means that the positive effect of all the levels of the happiness hormones in their daily lives cannot counteract the effects of cortisol, which has also been proven to be very harmful to our health when segregated continuously and at elevated levels, especially for the circulatory system and the acceleration of aging.

To better illustrate how stress can manifest in a person's life, I created a list of thoughts associated with the stress people under the *Cage Dreamers'* group may be experiencing in the working environment.

- "I'm going to be late again with this traffic,"
- "I have a meeting I did not prepare for very well,"
- "My boss is going to tell me again that we are not invoicing enough,"
- "I won't have time to make it to my husband's birthday dinner today,"
- "I may get fired because I screwed up in front of the client again."
- "I don't want to be scolded in front of the board."
- "My performance evaluation won't meet the expectations. As a result, I won't be promoted."
- "We won't meet the deadline and my boss will think fault, and not the lack of resources."

- "Nooo, it is Sunday again; I don't want to deal with my boss and coworkers tomorrow."
- "I am not ready to lead this project. I think they are trying to sabotage me."
- "They are downsizing the company; I will be the next laid off."
- "I am tired; I don't want to do this anymore."
- "They don't value my opinion, especially my boss, who always ignores me."

If you notice, most of these thoughts are based on fear and come with feelings of frustration, distress and insecurity, as if the stress was the impulse of the little voice in your head telling you that you are in constant danger, in a place where you don't feel safe, and at any minute, a tragedy or accident will happen. When these thoughts and feelings drive you, your body produces cortisol constantly, which keeps you in an automatic state of alarm and defensiveness—ready to fight or react violently. If this overall sensation of fear plays a leading role in your life, at some point, you will feel like you are living a nightmare from which it is impossible to wake up, something that today is what is broadly known as burnout.

For our benefit, there are natural methods and habits to cope with the sensation of anxiety and stress and control burnout, which you will learn in chapters 11 and 12. But, for now, it is fundamental to start creating awareness of your human nature and how this condition affects your well-being. Moreover, this understanding sets a tone of truth that is difficult to dismiss and also opens the door to a new universe — the power of your body's biology.

We have already learned that the fears and the stress ruling our lives come not only from the disgust we feel from our jobs today but are influenced by the variety of programs we have learned from our childhood and ancestors. On top of that, the combination of this collective consciousness with the physical reaction as consequence of millions of years of our bodies' evolutionary process also play an essential role.

However, the influence of our intrinsic biological design is way superior to the mere cultural and mental transformation — at least for hundreds of thousands of years. For example, if the early homo sapiens were walking on earth 250,000 years ago, and the industrial revolution started 250 years ago, we would have been suffering the pressure of the modern employment system for only 0.1% of our history. Moreover, most evolution happened outside the characteristics of the current civilization, meaning that our bodies were never designed to suffer the consequences of many situations the working world demands today.

For example, ancient communities did not have to suffer the judgment of hundreds of strangers during their lifetime. For thousands of years, communities were formed by few people, probably with a leader or two, and most knew each other.

However, today we are constantly exposed to the judgment of hundreds of individuals that are not even related to us — hundreds of kids in our school or college classrooms, dozens of coworkers and more than 500 friends on Facebook and LinkedIn. And although you would think this will help maintain high levels of serotonin and oxytocin, the hormones of acceptance and empathy, in current social conditions, being subjected to critics and judgment is way more common than admiration. For younger generations especially, when you are not liked on social media and don't build deep human interaction, the serotonin and oxytocin levels will decrease, becoming a critical factor of a depressive society.

Nowadays, we are exposed to a wild business environment. Even when our lives are not in danger, our brains and body react as if we were. We have automatically transferred the "fight or fly" instinctive reaction managed by cortisol and adrenaline to the business place. For example, people who give public speeches in front of thousands or present complex projects in front of clients and boards may feel exactly what cavemen did when a pack of wolves was hunting them. Being in unknown territories is also a factor for stress and cortisol release.

Additionally, if you are not motivated by great causes and have massive support from the people around you, the effects of cortisol can be harmful and even deadly. For example, I am sure that people like Martin Luther King Jr., who had a bigger goal than himself and was loved by many, are more motivated by serotonin and dopamine than mere survival instincts, as most people in the business world today.

There are many factors you should consider to keep the engine and the energy of your human nature performing. If some of those factors are out of alignment, your motivation could deteriorate at levels that can mislead your thoughts, reaching a point of desperation in your job and life. To keep yourself encouraged, making an income and liking what you do is never enough. What you do in your life should include many other characteristics, such as purpose and meaning, challenging goals and visible progress, the understanding that you are part of something bigger than yourself and your role in it, and a tribe you trust and unconditionally support you. Essential characteristics of happiness, you now know, are not psychological but biological.

The Values of a Firm

Many people I interviewed agreed that it is challenging to have all the conditions to be happy in a single place and that there is no such thing as a perfect job. Nevertheless, there are organizations and institutions with environments where you can feel safer, more valued and encouraged, compared to some traditional big corporations and firms where the modus operandi fosters the demotivation of their employees.

The evaluation system, for example, the checklist we spoke of in the first chapter used to review employees' performance, is a critical factor of demotivation. But, even when it can be a powerful tool to keep the *Visionary Followers* of the *Circle of Trust* committed; for others, this system is another discouragement tool that reminds you you are not good enough for the job. Like if you were in kindergarten and they told you your drawing was not as good as the others, to discover you were not as clever as your mother once told you. Yet, more than 30 years later, you are in the same position, constantly reminded of your incapability to excel at something.

The performance evaluation systems negatively affect many employees' motivation. But most corporations still don't understand that what they are implementing is, in fact, a very effective method to foster stress. Take, for example, the particular situation of a person who experienced shame and guilt during childhood. By implementing the evaluation system every year, he is reminded that he is not enough for the job he was hired for and works so hard. Regardless of whether he is or is not suited for the job, the system is triggering the same sensations of his childhood unconsciously, multiplying the level of anxiety instead of stimulating encouragement. The idea of mythological perfection expected of big corporations' employees was a time bomb that exploded during global governmental restrictions of 2020 and 2021 in the form of burnout, "the great resignation," and quiet quitting.

You cannot have an objective evaluation system managed by human beings that are also forgetting to consider a wide variety of soft skills needed to be a comprehensive professional, nor when the predominant evaluation system consists of comparing peers; no one can be equal and have the same skills as anybody else. However, when the DNA of many organizations in the corporate world is driven by financial growth instead of the growth of their people, we cannot expect otherwise. Regardless, now is the time to understand that not being equal doesn't mean that you are not a good professional or that you are not enough; it only means that your skills differ from the limited list defined by corporate policies.

This particular corporative characteristic reminds me of some of the typical partners' speeches when working for the firm: "We only have the best of the best, and only the best will stay." I wonder two things from this statement: first, if that was meant to threaten those who didn't have good performance reviews anticipating their dismissal, and second, if they believed from the bottom of their hearts that this was the truth. Nobody had probably told them that people who stay are just *Visionary Followers*, willing to sacrifice their lives to reach the *Promised Paradise* —nothing more, and not necessarily the best. It is time for leaders to change this old-fashioned way of speaking that may disregard some employees' esteem and hopes instead of motivating them.

In addition, as the performance review methodologies typically compare one employee to another, they foster a competitive vibe. Even when this may sound positive, everyone is pulling toward personal success in these environments, and no one is motivated to push the team's success. If, for example, we compare this situation with the first small communities of our civilization, they had to hunt and harvest together and protect the well-being of everyone to ensure the sustainability of the tribe. Living in an environment of trust was necessary to overcome inhospitable weather and threats from neighboring tribes. In communities where everyone has personal agendas—"sell a billion dollars to become a partner," "buy my own house to be accepted by others," or "prove to my boss that *I'm the best of the best*"— it is difficult to maintain a friendly atmosphere.

A way to create genuine and safe environments is to have the appropriate leaders. Today big corporations and firms don't need more "managers." They don't need heads of departments who follow orders and plans or comply with the skills of a checklist. That was for industrial revolution times. Today, we need leaders— people who are authentic pioneers, generate trust and inspire others. I have witnessed, gathered from my research and proved, working with my clients, that teamwork is authentic only when extraordinary leaders create an environment of trust, inspiration, and admiration. Environments where personal agendas could exist, but the unified goal is way more important for the entire team.

We were designed to be a social species with a collective objective and a cooperative purpose. And the business world and this civilization will not flourish if individuals keep pulling only for selfish benefits. We are still in time to learn the lessons we need to impact the world positively. It is our responsibility.

Personal story - A Savage Environment

This story tells how leaders did the opposite of creating trust.

Once, two of my bosses and I were in the middle of a meeting with one of the biggest and most profitable clients for the firm. I was explaining why what the client believed was part of the project was outside the scope and not our responsibility. We never offered that service, and we did not have the expertise to implement it. After I presented our situation as a firm, the client's project manager started yelling at me, exposing how tired she was of consultants like me and wanting me off the project. I was shocked by her reaction because I had never had that much contact with her. Plus, I did not understand why she was putting all the pressure on me when I only was communicating our team's position.

But what surprised me the most was the reaction of my bosses. They did not say a word, they did not support my presentation, and they did not defend me. For them, it seemed more critical not to face a client losing her temper than empathy for me. Even when I had successfully delivered the project for months, keeping an unreasonable client happy was way more important than the employee putting her "sweat and tears" on nights and weekends. As both supervisors were in very high positions on the project and the firm, their personal agendas to be partners were more important than the simple agenda of my "human nature" —to be respected and valued by my leaders. My trust in my so-called leaders ended that day. And I learned I deserved to be in a better, at least an environment where my supervisors had my back.

At the end of the meeting, I held my breath, left the room and broke into tears in the next available office. That day was the last time I cried before quitting that job for good.

...

Corporations are businesses, and many believe that the most critical responsibility of a business is to make a profit, as the economist Milton Friedman said in his famous article in the New York Times in 1970. This statement makes sense because the means to pay employees wouldn't exist without a profit. However, this thought closes the window for considering the most valuable stakeholder for corporations —their people's well-being, which embraces a much broader spectrum besides money. If big firms keep putting profit and clients before the employees, the result can be catastrophic to the business itself. That creates unmanageable staff turnovers to barely sustain an operation with unmotivated people.

We know that many firms and big corporations have implemented programs to improve their employees' quality of life, which highly consists of monetary benefits. But as we learned, our human nature also has other needs, such as belonging. People want to feel safe in their business environment and have leaders who have their backs in moments of crisis. They want to feel helpful, to work for a purpose and be good at what they do. Unfortunately, most companies depreciate the most essential of their assets by ignoring those profound needs. People are not corporations; even when they require money to survive, they need other aspects of their life to be balanced to achieve happy and fulfilling lives.

To summarize, firms and most big corporations have created systems driven by "values" that demerit good professionals, foster competition among team members and promote individualistic goals. These situations create a combination of biological and chemical reactions in our bodies with catastrophic consequences for our health and state of mind. And while this is not consciously premeditated, corporations still deny that their employees, before thriving lawyers and accountants, are human beings driven by the human nature of their minds, physiology and evolution.

Your Personal Values

Going deeper to understand the main motivations in your life, you will connect with memories of your professional life drivers. You will start remembering how you decided on your college major; go back to the moment, place and time when you defined what you wanted to become and remember what the drivers you considered in the decision-making process:

- Was it the likelihood of employment in your country?
- Was it fashionable at that moment?
- Was it the same path picked by your high school best friend?
- Was it the same career as your uncle Mark?
- Was it the same career as your mother?
- Was it something you dreamed of doing since you were a child?
- Or was it something that just came up in a Sunday afternoon conversation?

Remembering how I decided to become an engineer fills me with excitement. However, it was not a career I had always thought about pursuing. During middle school, for example, I wanted to be an architect. Although it was not something that suddenly came to my mind, my mother used to say that I would be excellent at it. This idea was reinforced by the high school career counselor, who confirmed I had spatial aptitudes, a skill that architects needed.

However, when the moment of truth arrived, everybody around me started commenting on my decision. I remember this moment like I was in the middle of a kids' movie like *Bee Movie*, *Antz* or *Boss Baby*, to name a few, where the moment you are born, "society" decides what you will do for the rest of your life. Even when this makes sense because the market has limited career offers—we all want to be employed, it does not make sense when you renounce what your soul profoundly desires.

My father said I should become a lawyer; my aunt said we don't need many architects in this city; my mother said I should do as my sister since she was doing great. But deep down, I was the only one who knew what I wanted, and it wasn't architecture. There was one thing that gave me joy and made my heart beat faster—science and astronomy. I dreamt, likewise many kids, of working for NASA. However, in my town, we never heard about famous scientists or research budgets from the government. Even today, no career is called 'space science' or 'astronomy.' It was almost laughable to think about becoming a planetary scientist. It was only the dream of a child.

I'm not a scientist yet, and I still don't work for NASA, but if someone who had a significant influence in my life would have said, "of course, you can make it to NASA," I swear to you I would be writing this book, probably with a different meaning, at my NASA's desk in Washington D.C.

I was only 17 and in the middle of adolescent confusion when I had to pick what to do with the rest of my life. This description sounds dramatic since we all know people commonly end up working in something they did not go to college for. But in my country, choosing your profession wisely is essential for your future. Choosing the right career will determine how you will live and how others will treat you. Where I come from, what you do for a living is a thermometer of "the good life," as we described in previous chapters, and it is directly related to your social status and the respect you will inspire in others. Unfortunately, our minds have been programmed to believe that if you pick a career that doesn't ensure money or decide not to go to college, you will surely be the next loser in town.

The fact that individuals in our civilization need to define their profession at such a young age is another product of the *invisible hand and the* establishment of the business world today. People are obliged to accommodate themselves to this "system" so they don't run behind compared to the rest of the population. However and despite certain current limitations, this generation, our generation, should feel very lucky. Decades ago, people didn't even have the opportunity to choose. There were not as many options in the market, and most people were destined to be farmers or continue the family business without question. Nevertheless, I wonder if that limitation in opportunities and information helped them to be happier or more comfortable with their lives. Current studies have concluded that unhappiness can also come from the excessive number of possible paths.

Continuing with identifying your values, think about the events that brought you to this moment in your career. Remember how you got your internship and current job and picked the company you are working for now. Then, identify which of these three different options describes your decision better.

The first option consists of consciously looking for a career, internship and a job position. You always knew you wanted to work for a specific company doing a particular job. Therefore, you did prepare yourself for years and applied for the job once, twice, or thrice until they welcomed you to the organization. The second option is synchronicities. You chose your career after a billboard you found walking downtown. Then, you were looking for a job, and a chain of events unfolded for you to find a job vacancy, apply and be accepted. Finally, the third option is fate. You were not considering anything similar to what you ended up doing, nor working for a firm or a big corporation. However, destiny found you; somebody offered a position, and you simply took the opportunity. The main difference between the three options is the intensity with which you picked your job —the first one being certain of what you wanted; the second one, one day you suddenly picked what you wanted, and your job is related to what you studied, and the third one had absolutely nothing to do with what you wanted in life.

Understanding how you reached this point in your professional career may set the tone for what you are looking for in life, your values, motivations and fears. For example, if you reached this point knowing that you were meant to be a Merger and Acquisition partner in a recognized firm, you went to law school and looked for a job among the top five law firms, you are a goal-oriented person who knows where to go. Today this means that as the clarity of the chosen path seems to vanish, looking for something different may feel terrifying. But, instead, if you were always told what to do, sent to an accounting school by your parents, and offered a job in a company that you didn't even know existed; and the fact that you had external little voices choosing your path, proves that a radical change is a natural path for your life. In addition, this situation also says about your attitude towards your life or, at least, why you feel so disappointed at your job.

The previous statements don't mean people are always happy whenever they consciously pick a career or a job. I have known coworkers and clients who have the fortune of loving what they do, even when they did not consciously look for it. The synchronicities in their lives showed them the way. On the contrary, others who thought they knew exactly what they wanted as a profession and defined plan found in their late 30s that they were unsatisfied with their jobs. But when you didn't consciously choose what you wanted, it may seem logical the need for a change. The variables to understand the business world, and how you prepared for it are infinite, therefore we will keep digging deeper to assimilate it.

Understanding why you picked a career or a job is not to feel disappointed or to blame others. Life put you here at this very moment for a reason, and all the things you have passed through and the situations you have overcome until today are essential pieces of the puzzle of your life. So, accept it, love it and feel thankful for it. However, understanding your motivations is also very important in learning more about yourself before defining a new game plan for the rest of your life.

Now that you are more aware of how you defined your career path, you understand better how your body works in terms of your energetic friends —hormones and neurotransmitters, which power you from the bottom of your natural existence, and you are more conscious about the values of the corporate world pulling you in other direction of your human nature, you can start focusing all of your attention towards the values in your own life. Your values are like your personal code of ethics; those aspects of your life you are not willing to negotiate. When you negotiate your values, you are playing against yourself — your truth, the life of your dreams, your family and your community.

Another important reason to define personal values is to understand that the "values" of the company you work for— if we can call them values— may contradict your own values. As a result, you will be trapped if you don't consciously separate both; you will never feel integrity, and your soul will feel defeated most days and for the rest of your life.

Exercise – Identifying Your Values

Now is the time to define and make a list of your values, but before you do a Google search of values, please think on your own and consider all the factors you identified in previous exercises—

your "dislikes" and emotions, your fears and escapisms, and the motivations you considered when you picked your career and your current job.

If the list exceeds 20 values, try to group them and define the top 5 most important ones. Next to each value, write down the dislikes, fear or escapisms, and hormones you think are most related to that value. Then, have an inner conversation about why you are running off something and not following your heart's desires. Finally, specify the changes you feel you need to make in your life and job to live those values continuously.

Value	Dislikes Fears/Escapisms Hormones	Life's Changes
Do something meaningful with a legacy for my team, community, and planet.	**Fear:** Have an unworthy life. **Escapism:** Using the weekends to party and watch television. **Hormone:** Serotonin	1. Start a business with purpose. or 2. Find a company whose values are similar to mine.

	Discussion: Even when my life does not need a justification to have value, I want to make the best of it, not only for me but for others.	

These values are your life code. They depict your essence and are your purest inner guide, like a life compass. With this exercise, you will start identifying which aspects of your life are not in alignment with yourself, so your decisions stop being based on fear and start coming from love. In the next chapter, we will evaluate other aspects of your life that you have yet to consider and keep aligning your life with what you really are.

Chapter 6 – Measuring Equilibrium

"A balanced and skillful approach to life, taking care to avoid extremes, becomes a very important factor in conducting one's everyday existence."

- Dalai Lama XIV -

So far, we have identified your dislikes, fears and values, entering the fourth layer of the *Matryoshka Method*. Hopefully, you have started to see some patterns and similarities among the exercises, and you have started to see the relationship you have with your job more clearly. You know now that your ancestors, how you were raised, how you decided your career and your human body play an important role in the relationship with your current work environment. However, in this chapter, you will step outside your job and profession and concentrate on other aspects of your life. Life should be balanced, and it's imperative to be aware of the status of those aspects before moving forward. What you do to make a living is just a piece of the puzzle of your reality. Unfortunately, most people only focus all their energies on something that did not even exist before the industrial revolution— employment—forgetting essential aspects for a joyful life.

The other aspects of a balanced life are money, immediate family, romantic relationships, adventure and fun, surroundings, body and health, social life and community, relationship with nature, art and creativity, intellectual and rational development, and spirituality and purpose. These aspects are my proposal for a balanced life, but each person could define as many as they think they need. For example, if you love charity and participating in NGO activities is essential for your life, you could create an independent category for it and not necessarily be contained in the category of social life and community. Similarly, if golf is a passion and is a place where most of your exercise happens, it could have an independent category and not necessarily be part of body and health.

However, before you enter to understand and evaluate your life balance, I will describe every proposed aspect to open the spectrum of your current beliefs and cultural programs. Your ideas for every aspect may be limited or have pessimist or negative thoughts holding you back, so we must decant them first.

It is important to know that this balance is essential because everything is connected within our psyche. Therefore, we cannot rip apart our happiness and well-being into pieces or parts as we can with a sheet of paper. When a part of your life is harmed, or you do not give enough attention to it, your mind still runs in the background, the effects of that deficiency affecting your entire life. And even when we cannot invest the same amount of time in every aspect due to the current circumstances of our lives, we need to make sure that we invest quality time in everything.

Money

We all know that money doesn't buy happiness, but it also gives us a lot of tranquility when available and solves most of the problems people think they have. Money is so important that it may be the only reason you go to work every day and sacrifice your freedom and deepest heart desires. It is the biggest concern for most people because it represents the means to survival and your status in the social pyramid.

I want to start exploring money with *real scarcity*. If money scarcity is a fact in your life—you have unbeatable debt, you are always short at the end of the month, and you have trouble taking your family on vacation or to a special place for the weekend, your current situation may likely be the same as what your parents or the person who raised you experienced when they were younger. Open your heart and be as honest as possible with yourself. Being thankful to your parents for all that they gave and the sacrifices they made for you, and the fact that you were not part of the poorest of the world doesn't mean that you have a good relationship with money. Don't get me wrong; thankfulness is crucial to attracting money. But still, if money is a constant concern in your life today and was a constant concern in your parent's life when you were a kid, you learned the scarcity program from them or your ancestor; therefore, you are unconsciously rejecting wealth.

And this doesn't mean that you are the erratic exception. But, as we have discussed before, you absorbed most of the programs from your childhood surroundings, and your parents and the people you grew up with play a leading role. So why do you think poor people who win the lottery often return to becoming poor? Or how do wealthy people that lose everything recover very easily and become rich again? This is because mindsets of scarcity repeal money, and mindsets of wealth attract money.

The second situation for continuing to explore money is the anxiety created around money when you don't have a real money shortage. Still, it is your biggest concern and occupies 80% of your thoughts. In other words, when you have everything you need to have "the good life" to pay for your home, have international vacations, and pay for your children's school and have their future ensured; and yet you are concerned about money all of the time, you may also have a counterproductive relationship with it. This stress around money is causing excessive cortisol in your life and making you lose the sides about other matters like your well-being, loved ones, and life itself.

Whatever your case may be: real scarcity or unnecessary anxiety, creating awareness about the possible unconscious beliefs you stored about money is vital to reprogramming a new mindset of abundance and improving your relationship with it. Let's commence by answering the following questions to unlock additional hidden limiting beliefs and give yourself a new opportunity and a fresh beginning.

- Was money abundant when you grew up?
- What does your religion say about money?
- What did your parents say about money when you were a kid?
- What do you think did people assume about your financial situation when you were little?
- How does your family refer to the poor, and how do they refer to the rich?
- What does your parents say about money today?
- Do you think that working hard is the only way to make money?
- Do you believe having tons of money is bad and only possible when you are dishonest?
- Do you believe some people have more money because they steal from the poor?
- Do you count every penny you expend?

- Do you invest in yourself, or is everything for survival or emergency savings?
- Do you expend everything you earn and never think about your future and the people around you?
- Do you value money as an important aspect of life, or is it secondary?
- Do you always buy the cheapest detergent for your clothes, or are softness, good smell and quality more important?
- Do you believe people with much money should give it to the poor and not buy things for themselves?
- Do you always owe money to other people, and haven't you paid your debts on time?

After answering these questions, I want to clarify that a positive appreciation for money is also necessary. Money is a form of energy used to exchange for the things we need to have a good life and experience new things. But if you believe that money is evil and is only about greed, or your religion and parents did think so, there is an additional program to consider. The relationship with money should be like the relationship with the other aspects of your life. It is not about rejection, fear or lust or greed. It is about nurturing these aspects in a way that does not feed negativity or victimhood but instead helps you grow and expand your quality of life.

If you are thinking about money too much, not because you appreciate the value of money but because of scarcity, or the fear of losing your current status, you need to understand that worrying about money won't bring more money. So, I have different proposals for a positive change in this relationship.

First, define a moment per week or preferably per month to sit down, pay down your bills, and prepare a budget for the next period. Like this, you will consciously think about money only once a month, so you can open space and attention to other important things, like having quality time with your family and yourself or working on the business you always ambitioned.

Secondly, suppose you don't have real issues with money but are still constantly scared and complain about how expensive everything is. In that case, I recommend you start having a thankful relationship with it. For example, every time you pay a bill, pay for dinner and help a relative in trouble, change the feeling of anxiety for a feeling of gratitude, and say loudly—"thank you universe, because I have the money to pay and to help." When you have a positive relationship with money and spend and invest with a good heart, money will always find its way back.

Third, if you are afraid of debt, which is the case for many people, it is the same as being afraid of money itself. We all know some people end up paying more interest than for the goods, and sometimes people lose their homes or freedom due to their debt. So even when it is normal to be scared of interests, that is how they designed the system; it is unhealthy. Loans are simply a tool of the system that, if you learn how to take advantage of it, can open doors of incredible opportunities. Without a loan, many would not have gotten the things that made their life worth living or would not have experienced marvelous adventures that changed their lives. Yes, you may feel a little trapped when asking for a loan, but you are also losing opportunities due to a fear that will never materialize, especially when you are a responsible investor. I am not saying to be irresponsible with money; as we learned, it is essential to appreciate and value it to multiply it. I suggest you educate yourself to prevent your financial life from becoming a snowball that will consume everything you have instead of becoming a snowball of opportunities and abundance.

Money and debt are tools that help us move in this tridimensional world, and we need them today in our civilization. In the past, there was no money, and in the future, we don't know if the concept of money will be the same—time, water, information, or ideas could just as well become how we trade. Money is an illusion in our 21st-century brains. So, stop putting all your energy and attention into papers with former presidents printed on them or digital zeros in your bank account. Instead, start valuing money for what it is and not as the epicenter of your life. A beautiful and happy life is not only about money. Many other important things are necessary to find inner peace. Let's discover what they are.

Immediate Family

Depending on where you are coming from, the relationship with your immediate family is critical for you to feel balanced. In some cultures, we have a relationship with our parents, siblings, and kids which are strong and deeply bound. In other cultures, those relationships are definitively less connected, and the contact with parents and siblings is probably once a year for Christmas.

Whatever the case, the relationship you had and have with your immediate family marks your life forever. As mentioned in chapter four, your brain is programmed by all the experiences, beliefs, and fears from previous and current generations while growing up. We are nothing more than the product of those relationships combined with millions of years of evolution.

However, your homework here goes beyond the physical connection you have with your family members, such as the number of calls per week, the number of messages per day, or the number of times you visit each other every year. Instead, the connection with each one of your family members can only be found inside yourself — your thoughts and feelings.

To understand this point better, do this exercise and think about your brother, your parents, dead or alive, observe the thoughts and connect with feelings for each one. What do you see? —love, compassion, anger, resentment, envy, hope, affection, judgment or admiration. Whether you observe positive or negative feelings, all the thoughts and emotions you have when thinking about your immediate family are nothing more than reflections of you; they are your clearer mirror. Like it or not, you also have important pieces of what they are inside your psyche. You would be lying to yourself whenever you deny this deep connection. Moreover, if you want to balance out the pieces of your life and heal the relationship with your family, negative feelings and thoughts towards them must surface in your conscious mind so that you can discern and reflect on them.

If you feel resentment, frustration or anger arousing when thinking about a family member, I recommend doing two things. First, understand that whatever you feel has more to do with you than with them. It's just an impression of an unconscious fear projected in your mind. It is an interpretation of reality and does not necessarily mean it is true. Therefore, instead of creating a direct judgment against that person, try to see if fears come to the surface. For example, you may fear acting like them, fear living their lives or a hidden memory of a childhood moment that you didn't know how to process. There is always a second layer within our psyche. Second, understand that whatever that person did, they thought they were doing their best for survival or their happiness. Like the rest of us, we normally act based on our unconscious fears

If you feel that it is impossible not to criticize or feel negative emotions toward certain family members, don't worry. In chapter 11, we will further discuss the unconscious mind and how to improve our relationships with others, and the meaning of the impressions you have within yourself

Note: *Don't judge or blame yourself if you have a dysfunctional family relationship. We are not obliged to have perfect relationships with our family members. In the end, even if we share many things, we can also choose different paths and believe in different things. The only thing that matters is how you feel about it. So, if you believe you need to do something to improve that relationship, do it—do not hesitate to take the phone and call them and fix it. But if you feel at peace and know your soul should be apart, that may be exactly what you need now. There is no recipe, and there is no one perfect way. Only you and only your heart will know the answers.*

Romantic Relationships

It took me decades to understand that a romantic relationship's success depends on two very connected realities. One is your relationship with yourself, and two is the energy level or your perception of life. I know you have heard this cliché, "If you don't love yourself, nobody will?". But as cliché as it may sound, it can be one of the most powerful sayings about the art of living. So, every time you do something to improve yourself, grow, and feel better about life, you are directly working on your relationship with your partner. And this book is no exception.

Everything you will learn here is helping with the relationship with yourself and the relationship with your current partner or your partner in the future.

We know that we have not been monogamous forever, but as we learn in our previous chapters is important to understand where this originated. Some anthropologists say that males started staying longer with the same female to take care of their offspring. Others say that females started accepting males in the entire cycle for the male to stay and protect them. Either way, today, this connection is vital for harmonious and balanced lives in many aspects: social, cultural, biological, and even energetic (as explained by Taoism with the yin-yang balance), which may apply not only to heterosexual couples but also to homosexuals since we all can manifest both energies. Whatever the reason is, our civilization chose monogamy over polygamy in most societies; this is the path that our collective consciousness has picked to evolve. As we can see now, your partner and the family you build with them are the building blocks of our society.

However, nowadays, many people have consciously decided to be alone. Many single people are convinced they don't need a partner to be happy or complete, but this can only be true if they don't deny the biological and psychological truths behind a family and the importance of having someone in their lives. The decision of loneliness always happens after bad experiences in previous romantic relationships. No one is born with the idea or the program that being alone is the best option for survival. This thought, as most of the content of our minds, is a program we learned from the culture and cultivated with our experiences. And denying the importance of the social bond with a partner also denies the essence of our species and existence. If people keep with the idea of solitude without considering they are betting against their mental health and happiness, it can bring additional unconscious pain and resentment. But, if this is your final decision, and what you want is to have a dog and two cats as companions instead of giving it a try to love, you must do deep inner work. This decision is never as simple as deciding what sweater to wear, and you must consciously work in yourself to heal and find inner peace in your life.

Now, take a moment to think about you and your current relationship or your previous relationships if you are single today, and answer the following questions.

- Is everything working as you expected, or is there always something wrong?
- Are the communication levels high with no secrecy involved?
- Do you trust each other and respect each other all of the time, physically and verbally?
- Do you have interests in common?
- Are you still passionate about each other?
- Is there a place you rather be than next to your significant other?

- Do you understand his or her needs, and do they understand yours?
- Do you settle with the reality of this relationship or are constantly working on improving it?
- Are you constantly afraid about the future of the relationship?

In addition to these questions, identify other aspects that may not be working or did not work in your previous relationships and link them to why they didn't work. Then identify trends in the world of possibilities of flaws and problems. All of the aspects you dislike of your romantic relationships and the reasons you are recognizing now, as everything we have discussed previously, reflect your unconscious beliefs and some of your fears.

However, it is not easy to see ourselves in this reflection and the accountability on our part. Because of the power romantic relationships have in our lives and the lack of understanding of our psyche, it is easy to become victims of the partner and the situation. And probably, your thoughts may sound like this:

- She did not love me as I expected
- He cheated on me, and that is all his fault.
- She dumped me because she is a spoiled woman.
- He never talked to me, and when he did, he lied
- She was not ready for commitment; she was a player.
- He was violent; He disrespected me most of the time
- She didn't know what she wanted; she was probably crazy

- He cannot be alone; He used me
- She is a bossy and unhappy woman
- He is a controlling man; I couldn't be free

Instead of sounding like this:

- I did know what I wanted; I misinterpreted the signs
- I became distant and silent; the magic died
- I was hoping he would end the relationship; I didn't want to take that responsibility
- I wasn't completely honest with myself; I didn't want to see the truth.
- I had been confusing attachment with love for so many years.
- I grew on a different path; we didn't have anything in common anymore.
- I didn't take the time to know him before deciding to be together.

Few times do we take responsibility as an active part of the relationship. But taking responsibility is not taking the blame or believing we are not enough to be loved. Instead, taking responsibility is a work we start doing by understanding how the mind works and how this affects the communication and the reality between two people. It is about understanding your deepest fears and massively acting to heal what is making you suffer. When people ignore the conditions of the mind, by default, they blame the first thing they see, which is generally the person next to them. Additionally, as relationships are constructed by two people who continuously exchange energy, emotions, and thoughts, our partners become the primary mirror of ourselves and show us precisely what we are afraid of confronting — our deepest shadows. This situation makes relationships the main driver of our inner healing, giving it an additional meaning for growth and spirituality, to heal and recuperate the trust in ourselves.

There is an additional and fundamental aspect of relationships which is called polarity. Even when I could write an entire book about this topic because it is complex and often misinterpreted, still, I will touch on this topic here, so you can start making discernment around your relationships with the opposite sex. Polarity is the balance needed for two opposite forces to coexist without overcoming one of the two. This polarity is present in all of the phenomena of the universe; for example, darkness cannot exist without light, and the concept of heat only makes sense when there is also cold. For many ancient cultures, this polarity is the origin of the universe; and what is contained in it, like life itself. Most of these cultures have also used the concept of polarity to describe the energy in the masculine-feminine relationship and state that for any relationship to coexist needs a balance of both; otherwise, a force will destroy the other, and the possibility of a harmonious relationship. Men and women were built differently and after a precise evolutionary process of millions of years. In essence, they have different roles in the survival of species. For more than we can do very similar things or have similar jobs, it is easy for a woman to do certain things and vice-versa. And this is not sexism, feminism or being pro of the patriarchy. This difference is only the state-of-the-art and the truth of our species. We are not equal.

However, many people have confused the human rights movement with the equality of the sexes and interpreted that both women and men should act, do and behave the same instead of comprehending that these movements were claiming just equality of rights. This confusion has not simply permeated the business world and the government but harmed the relationships between men and women. Many women, rather than potentializing the feminine energy traits to balance the difference, started claiming their place in society and demanding respect from the patriarchy by using masculine attributes, the obvious reaction of a western culture that doesn't understand energy. Many women didn't know how to unleash their intrinsic feminine energy then, and many women don't know how to do it today. Likewise, many men didn't know how to unleash their intrinsic masculine energy then, and many don't know how to do it today—creating a snowball effect that has irreversibly affected families, relationships and marriages for the last 50 years. For example, one of the reasons for this negative effect is that men unconsciously felt they lost the purpose of protecting and taking care of their families— a biological and undeniable characteristic of the adult human male evolution. Another reason is the excessive masculine behaviors in women, which take them away from their feminine natural energy, which creates additional pressure on the female system, prevents energy from flowing naturally in their bodies, and provokes stress and anxiety.

The lack of polarity in romantic relationships leads to a blurred, undefined or unbalanced dynamic, resulting in boredom, lack of excitement, and loss of intimacy. This confusion can also cause dissatisfaction in the relationship as each partner ignores their specific role or what is expected of them, leading to misunderstandings and difficulties in communication. Finally, it will lead to a lack of direction and purpose in the relationship, negatively impacting its overall health and longevity.

Within the spiritual coaching community, however, there is still some disagreement on the characteristics of a balanced relationship. It is hard to leave behind the war of the sexes installed in our minds for decades. With the remaining superficial discussions, reaching a middle ground between our biological evolution and our cultural development will be challenging. It will take time, and a lot of energy for thinkers like me, to find the space where modern psychology and neuroscience meet the metaphysical discussion around energy. However, any profound transformation starts with self-knowledge, which is one of the goals of this book.

Note: Please, if you have decided to be alone and made a conscious decision, do not believe there is no hope for your happiness. As we exposed here, having a beautiful relationship with yourself is the way you balance this aspect of your life. Yes, you may not have the great mirror, but with time will make find healing all around in and from every other person who comes into your life.

Adventure and Entertainment

It is also possible to write an entire book about the importance of adventure. And when I say adventures, I'm not necessarily saying to go and embrace Mount Everest's quest or skydiving. Instead, the little adventures are the thermometer to measure how you envision your life and embrace the amazing opportunity of being alive. If, for example, you are most of the time in the same place, street, house, routine, and around the same people, you are probably afraid of something, or you may be afraid of life itself. On the contrary, if you like continuously going to new places, meeting new people, driving for a different route, and joining a new group, you are willing to face new challenges and explore new versions of yourself. A starting point to find passion, purpose and reinvention.

Remember that having an adventurous life has little to do with money. So do not bring these excuses of your fearful mind to the table. Adventure comes from the willingness to explore the world, but overall to explore who you are and what you want in this life. You only need creativity, imagination and passion to start leaving your comfort zone. And as I say at the beginning of this topic, it does not have to be extravagant adventures. Gradual changes to your day and your routine can positively and enormously impact your life—like a butterfly effect.

Whatever your situation is, I challenge you to go this week and embrace a new adventure. Go to a beautiful national park, join a group on something you want to learn or go to a class on whatever you have been curious about for a long time. Instead of spending next Sunday watching a marathon on Netflix, charge your batteries with a new adventure. You don't need money; you don't need to invest more time; you only need a little creativity. If you think creativity is not your thing, ask Google or ChatGTP; there is an answer most of the time.

Surroundings and physical environment

I also want you to start being more aware of your surroundings. When I mean surroundings, please include where you spend more of your time and the people around you. They say you are the average of the five people you share most of your time with. And it makes sense. The energetic field you are moving in is charged with the same level of energy that you have. Insecure and unpleasant places or pessimistic people directly affect your thoughts, ideas, beliefs and moods.

It is important to understand that you don't need to be attached to the same places and the same friends, but this also takes a lot of discernment because it is hard to be objective when you are fully immersed in something that is not beneficial for the soul. This idea does not necessarily mean that you must move to another town and delete your closest friends from your phone. But consider that staying in the same place for many years, surrounded by the same people, is the exact reason you haven't found your tribe, purpose or the life you desired.

Starting today, cultivate curiosity about the places you want to be, the restaurants you want to go to, the vacations you want to have, and the people you want to become. Look around you and ask yourself where you may find them. Then, call that old acquaintance you believe is having the life of your dreams, someone you believe can be a role model or person who has had the transformation you desire. And it is simple; you only need to ask them to share their experience with you. Most people are eager to share their transformational journeys.

Join new groups, in person or online. There are groups for everything and everyone. Just pick the topic you feel inspired about, or try to find a group related to a new business idea or a new quest or adventure you want to commence. In these groups, you will connect with new thoughts, mindsets, and experiences, but overall, you will start understanding that what you want is possible; others have already made it. Opening your energetic field to new people and places will bring a lot of new inspiration and ideas.

Finally, look around your house. Is this the home you always wanted, and how should it look? If not, start identifying what you don't like and how you think you can change it. The changes can vary from organizing the closet, cleaning the kitchen or painting the walls to remodeling your house, changing the neighborhood or finally leaving your grandmother's house. Where you spend most of your time is vital for you to feel better. More space, more light, a better view, and less noise have massive positive impacts on how you feel. Your house's environment directly impacts how you feel, the balance of your hormones and your relationship with the external world — your partner, your children and your work.

Don't limit your ideas here, either. Instead, be positive and start looking for a change regardless of what your thoughts tell you. Sometimes making the decision is everything it takes to start acting and sending the right messages to the Universe. If your limitation is money, a leasing contract, or the fear of being far from your family, ignore it. Don't let that prevent you from looking for the change that can impulse your exponential growth. The opportunities when you are ready to move appear in the less imaginable places.

Personal Experience: I have been traveling and working with my husband for around two and a half years. We have lived in around twelve different places and have twelve different relationships, meaning that the feelings and emotions around the

relationship are different in every place we arrive. For example, the relationship deteriorates when apartments are dark and noisy, and we don´t feel in harmony with the place. Instead, the relationship flourishes when we like the town and the apartments are new, spacious and clean. The moment we identify the place does not make us feel secure and happy; we immediately start looking for a better one. I am sure this has been one of the keys to our relationship and inner balance.

Body and Health

Body and health are, without a doubt, one of the most important aspects of your life. It is the instrument you use to do everything— loving and caring for others and going to work. However, it is a complex vessel with many variables and interconnections, many of which are still waiting to be discovered and understood by scientists. Yet, regardless of this complexity, with the information we know today, there is much room for deciding what is best for it to function properly.

The human body is the container of eleven major organ systems and trillions of cells communicating tons of information per second. The communication among cells affects biological functions like digestion and breathing and is also accountable for our mood changes and thoughts. Unfortunately, people often ignore the importance of the link between the mind, how we feel, and the body. This ignorance reinforces the idea that the only important thing around healthy dieting and exercise is how they look from the outside. In other words, the only important thing is their fat and muscle percentage and how sexy they look to others, creating a culture of irresponsible dieting and cosmetic surgery.

On the other hand, we have people who don't even care about how their body looks. Rather, they have created a culture of excessive eating and consumption, like poisoning their bodies with excessive animal fats, sugars, alcohol, and cigarettes were, in fact, sexy. Anyway, in both cases, people usually only care about their health when they get sick, feel physical pain or end up in the ER.

I can't help but wonder how a person with current knowledge about the importance of a healthy diet and the danger of certain substances still irresponsibly starves themselves in diets, smokes or eats excessive sugar and saturated fat. Is it because they ignore the link between this behavior with deadly illnesses like cancer, diabetes, inflammation and hormone unbalance? Or if they know this, why isn't this knowledge enough to control physical addiction? Let's try to find out.

Some of these behaviors are believed to be related to the unconscious desire to die, like a slow suicide. For example, some scientific evidence has shown a direct relationship between smokers and suicide and has statistically proven that smokers are more likely to kill themselves than non-smokers. This theory, however, doesn't prove that there is a desire to die. It only proves that smoking is the expression of lack, an inner void that needs to be filled. For example, if we had the technology to predict the probability of a particular person getting lung cancer or diabetes, a smoker or a compulsive sugar eater would be more likely to stop. But as doctors cannot be sure they will get sick, it is easy for an unsatisfied mind to choose the artificial dopamine rush than overthinking what may happen in the future. So more than a desire to die is a bet against time and the escapism from a feeling.

Other recent research on animal food disorders has shown that bad bacteria stored in their guts directly communicate with their brains. Bad bacteria may be responsible for sending the brain the signal to crave sugars and junk food. The gut directly connects to the brain, not through simple neurotransmitter release, as believed before, but through the enteric nervous system. A network of nerve cells lining the digestive tract that has been called "The second brain." This system contains a complex neural net that can work and make decisions independently and controls the main digestive system functions. This communication channel between the gut and the brain goes both ways, which means that your moods are directly linked to your gut and the other way around. For example, we all have experienced or know that when people have a traumatic experience feel sick and instantly feel nauseous and vomit. In addition, when mental distress lingers for years, it exacerbates the overall functioning of the digestive system in the long term and metabolism—vital for the control of your weight and your overall health.

Understanding this direct connection can be obvious for many people, but it has not been obvious for previous generations. Therefore, we keep many harmful cultural eating behaviors and other attitudes that foster stress without understanding the effects on our mental and physical health. It is important to acknowledge that whatever you decide to put in your body and do with it is one of the few things you can control in your life today. This statement means that the options to understand the importance of our body and access to healthy food are your responsibility and are only restricted to people who live in the middle of the jungle or a desert in Africa without internet access. But you do not have excuses. You can access the information you need to change your habits and the luxury of visiting the grocery store down the street and choosing among thousands of healthy options.

Unfortunately, many still pick the sugary donut instead of kale and blueberries. Well, it is not a secret that addictions, obesity and stress are still very common and rising, like the discoveries of science and technology of the 21st century were not enough to assimilate what is good or bad for your mind and body. One of the most powerful reasons for this behavior is the unconscious mind, the part of ourselves we cannot perceive, and that is independently making decisions for us. In other words, even when people consciously know what is harmful, unconscious beliefs, toxic programs, harmful habits and cultural behaviors win the battle of what to consume.

Gratefully, this book has been designed to understand your unconscious mind and start winning this battle. The previous chapter and the following ones will give you tools to start implementing new habits and reprogramming your mind. It does not make sense that you are the most important person for yourself and are not yet making the right decisions. In chapter twelve, for example, we will better understand how to change and improve your habits. But, for now, creating awareness is enough to measure the equilibrium in your life.

Community and Social Life

We will only spend a little time talking about this topic, as we already saw in previous chapters, and how our human nature has evolved through the formation of tribes and social bonds for the survival of our species. We are social beings, and our nature requires us to identify a place to belong, where we feel proud to be a part of and feel valued. However, today the representation of that ancient tribe has mutated a little. For some people, it may be the church; for others, it may be work and the office; for others, a soccer team or volunteer work.

If this is your case and you feel you have not found a place you belong, where you feel safe, and that gives you a sense of purpose, you may have found one of the main reasons for your dissatisfaction in life. Anyway, when you start exploring life, as I mentioned before, through new adventures and connecting to new people that inspire you, you will start understanding better who you are and where you want to stay. When you decide to belong and consciously start this exploration journey, places, people, and new communities will magically show up in your life. You only need to connect with your current desires and your intrinsic creativity. Nevertheless, I will give you some ideas.

If, for example, you don't participate in any community services or volunteer work, sign up today or tomorrow. Find a cause that moves you, something that has been calling you for a long time, but you moved to the bottom of your to-do list because you believed it was not a priority. However, right now, you know its importance and the link there is for your balance and your mental health. If you cannot think of anything, give yourself a little time. Everyone with desires to help, has heard of a group they feel called to and have heard about a noble cause that resonated with them. You can also ask your friends so you can work together or google what social work and community services are needed in your town.

Reminder: *You don't need to share with the world what you do for others. The selfie with the starving kid in Africa means nothing but your ego making peace with unconscious guilt. So instead, please do it for yourself. Do it because you care, and you will feel better whenever you share your legacy and energy with others.*

Connecting with your friends and family is another way to create the bonds for a balanced life. Unfortunately, we lose many friendships because of our daily routines and automatic life modes. But it is interesting to recuperate them, especially as we get older. The bonds we believe with our youth friends are eternal; they are marked in our minds and transport us to moments when we were building our programs, beliefs and ideas about the world. Yes, we all change during our lifetime, and when we do the inner work, many of those points of view can change. However, not everything from childhood was negative, and the connection to that enjoyment can bring new nuances to our current life.

Of course, you don't have to force anything; it must feel natural. So take some time to think about which of your friends you want to be in contact with again and do it.

Your Relationship with Nature

When I first wrote the book, it did not include this section — Your Relationship with Nature — as part of a balanced life. However, I decided to add it after discovering the significance of contact with nature in your inner healing and overall well-being.

Many of us didn't have the fortune of growing up around nature but in the middle of concrete cities; therefore, we have the idea that nature is something far away you visit when you hike or are on vacation. This disconnection was exacerbated by television shows, both movies and documentaries, where it is common that a creepy creature always wants to hunt you or a terrifying shark that will ruin your vacation on a California beach. With time, the disconnection started to become fear, and nature not only became something we are not related to but an amorphous creature that will get you.

Then we got the environmental movement, and many naively believed that this was the hope for humanity and our reconciliation with nature. However, something even worse happened. The reconciliation with nature started to mutate to hate for humanity and became a war against ourselves and our civilization. Soon we started to hear that humans are a plague and that we are the ones who should disappear from the face of the earth. But even when it is understandable that it is in our hands to take care of nature and that we need to act faster than ever, despising humans won't solve anything. On the contrary, it will eliminate the imminent need for meaningful conversations to find real solutions. If something, taking care of nature can only come from our love for each other and our humanity, not from the fear of nature or the hate for other humans.

Improving how we treat the earth and its habitants start with taking responsibility for our actions and not blaming others. Again, I remind you that the *invisible hand* created the state of the art of the current civilization, and the people who started eating meat for survival, cutting trees down to build homes, and the ones who discovered how oil generates energy didn't do so thinking: "Yes, let's do this so we can destroy the planet." We are all the result of what happened in the past; therefore, blaming the past is not how we make peace with the present or change the course of our future.

I am optimistic; we are still on time, and mother-earth wisdom will do what it takes to bring the balance back to earth. And even when big corporations are pulling for their benefits and the renewable energy industry is now more interested in making money, forcing the implementation of still damaging solutions to nature. Nevertheless, human consciousness and technology are always evolving, so hopefully, not too far in the future, consciousness and technology will catch up and balance out to solve environmental issues and eliminate the Hollywood myth of having to escape from the earth we destroyed.

We are not only part of nature; we are made by nature. For this reason, the gradual disconnection from it and the lack of comprehension of its importance is one of the primary causes of modern illnesses like stress. Even when peace with nature may take some time, it is essential for a balanced life. For example, some European medical systems have already started to prescribe spending time in nature because of the positive impact on mental health and the notable reduction of stress and anxiety. They have also found that a break from technology and other modern distractions can help us increase mindfulness and self-awareness — fundamental characteristics of inner peace and calmness. Ultimately, what we can learn from this is not that nature will heal us from the toxicity of the modern world, but is actually our disconnection with it is making us sicker.

Please take a moment and think about your feelings regarding nature and your relationship with it:

- Do you fear nature, animals, water or any aspect of it?
- Do you dislike the countryside?
- Do you say to yourself that you are an urban person?
- How often do you go out of the city and visit nature?
- Do you get bored in nature?

Personal Experience: *I've been afraid of water since I can remember; so extreme that I could not be in a pool by myself. It is probably because I was born in the mountains and visited the sea only a couple of times when I was a kid. Some people also tell me it is because of my ancestral heritage, past lives, or astrological chart. But regardless of the reason, the fear was there, and I knew it was important to work on it. Everything in our mind is connected; the less fear we experience, the freer we can be. So, in 2022, I decided to work on that fear and started snorkeling thrice every week. After a couple of months, the fear did not disappear completely, but I didn't have to leave the water within the five first minutes. I developed a unique relationship with the sea and its life inside. If something, working on that fear released unconscious fear blocking me in other aspects of my life and opened one of the most valuable experiences to share with my partner. Now, I am back in* the mountains, but I cannot wait to return to the ocean. I miss the little fish a lot.

Art and Creativity

> "Art is stored creativity that decides to leave the dimension of the mind to be manifested in the physical world so it can be appreciated by the senses of other humans´ brains and store an impression. Therefore, art expressions transform the world as we know it to create perpetual human connections that transcend the dimensions of space and time."

If we compare ourselves with the rest of the primates, we share more than 98% of the DNA. This similitude means that we need similar characteristics for harmonious survival. They don´t need money or a professional career, but they need social and status interactions, sexual relationships, exercise and a healthy diet, as well as we do. However, when it comes to Art and Creativity, we are far from them. And even when it sounds little, this 2 % of the DNA that separates us from chimpanzees is where is found the development of human civilization — from the first cave painting, "The Odyssey" by Homer, and Beethoven's Symphony No. 9, to the Monalisa by Leonardo Davinci, and the Taj Mahal.

All the things found in our creativity, dreams, imagination, myths and how we express them, language and plastic arts, are essential for our modern life balance. Science has already confirmed the importance of artistic and creative activities like painting, writing, singing and acting. Engaging in any of these activities improves mood, self-esteem, and confidence. These results are also related to the increase in oxytocin and serotonin, which decreases the sensations of stress and anxiety and improves the overall well-being of the individuals.

It is like human beings were designed to create and experience art. Think, for example, of a three-year-old kid around loud, happy music or with watercolors. It is almost like an intrinsic impulse humans need for their personal development and the progress of our civilization. Most of what we are could not have been possible without these aptitudes.

However, many mistakenly believe that people must be as skilled as Beethoven or a genius like Leonardo Davinci to participate in any creative endeavor. This mistaken belief was planted decades ago when the education system used to sabotage the creativity of so many children. I hope they don't keep doing that today, and children can continue exploring their inner creative Michelangelo at the same level as mathematics and computing programming.

However, today, you are responsible for recovering that part of you that has probably been hiding for decades, especially if you don't have any creativity or art responsibilities at your job. If this is your case, look for a connection with your imagination and its materialization outside your office. The universe of creations and arts is infinite, and humanity has yet to discover millions of possibilities and manifestations of art. Imagine how many more poems, songs, movies, and paintings are waiting to be created from our imagination and collective consciousness, and you are part of this consciousness.

If you still think you are not creative or skilled in arts, please read this part of the book again, and try to understand that everyone was designed equally and with the same possibilities. Plus, even when you can paint and write a famous piece and live from the art, we don't need to consider that variable to create something new. To explore the hidden seed of creativity and art within you, you only need love for yourself.

If any of the typical examples of art I gave you in the previous chapter don't work for you as the manifestation of art, remember that art and creativity can be found anywhere:

- Painting your bedroom.
- Decorating for Christmas.
- Creating new recipes to cook for your family.
- Helping your entrepreneur girlfriend to design new sales flyers.
- Learning to sew and design your clothing.
- Going to museums and appreciating arts and their history.

- Going to live music and learning about new music styles.
- Decorating your home with a vintage style.
- Participating in the new office remodeling.
- Creating NFTs (which I still need to understand).
- Resume the ukulele classes you started in high school.
- Reading old poetry books after dusting them off.
- Writing the children's book, you always wanted.

Intellectual and Rational Development

Like creativity and arts, the intellectual and rational development dimension not only sets us apart from the rest of the primates but is what made us homo-sapiens-sapiens. Even when we know there are no biological differences between homo-sapiens and homo-sapiens-sapiens, the significant advances in technology and science and our culture's complexity are the main characteristics that describe the modern human. So intellectual and rational development is like an additional stepstone for a balanced life. It is a new archetype of our civilization and collective consciousness that we should cultivate.

One of the main reasons for cultivating this archetypal trait that previous homo sapiens 20,000 years didn't is the need to process the excessive amount of information that current humans are subjected to continuously. If humans do not develop critical thinking and analysis, the possibility of getting trapped in dogmas and fear is imminent. Rational thinking development and intellect are fundamental to improved decision-making, enhanced problem-solving skills, enriched communication, increased creativity and improved mental health.

Note: When measuring intellectual and rational development in your life, please don't consider newspapers or mass media. We know that those are polluted with political propaganda. Instead, go to the source and consider research magazines, books, book clubs, research documents, essays, going back to school, documentaries, literature, and independent journalism.

Spirituality and Purpose

Before I get to the explanation of this point, I want to clarify something. No matter if you are a religious person or you consider yourself an atheist. Being spiritual has nothing to do with omnipotent power or the existence of a soul that will transcend this world to the other. I don't have this answer, and nobody can prove that today. Spirituality and finding your life purpose are matters of being good humans, finding joy and completeness, and not a matter of finding the ultimate truth about God.

Spirituality is a philosophy of life that changes how you think and act. It is the breakpoint between the fear and the love we spoke about at the beginning of the book. It is a decision on how you want to embrace life and every little moment unfolding before your eyes. So the starting question of a spiritual journey is as simple as answering whether you want to continue living in fear and suffering because life is unfair or whether you want to be at peace with life despite the events you or others face. I'm not trying to say that you need to be apathetic or ignore what is happening around you. On the contrary, it is about becoming more aware and conscious about everything— the life in front of you and the love for yourself.

However, spirituality is hard to crack in our current society, and I need you to feel comfortable reading about it. So please, do not think you have just reached the voodoo and nonsensical part of the book. Before you close this and put it on the pile of unread books shelf, I want you to explore the following situation.

Imagine you are driving in a hurry, going late for work; you didn't even have time for breakfast. You have the first meeting is scheduled at 8 am and can only make it by 8:30 if traffic is good. It is a meeting you have been waiting for more than two months to close a deal with a potential client. Plus, it's very difficult to get an appointment with this person; she is very busy and frequently travels. You are going late because you were tired and didn't hear the alarm. Your next-door neighbor had a loud celebration after his football team won the finals the night before, and the celebration lasted until 3 am.

You run out of gas in the middle of the commute, and the car stops just before taking the exit on the highway. And that's when you remember that you were supposed to wake up earlier to go to the gas station in the morning, but in the middle of the rush, you forgot about it.

You know you cannot physically do anything to make it on time at this point. How would you react? More than thinking about what you would do, think about the sequence of events that would manifest in your mind and body. For you to understand me better, there are two ways your body-mind can react; one is from your unconscious mind, the fear side, or the second is the conscious mind, the love side.

The fear side would be releasing lots of cortisol and adrenaline. You would start sweating, and your heart would beat faster. Nevertheless, you don't even notice that reaction in your body because your mind is foggy, and you can only think about how angry you are with yourself because you forgot to stop for gas. Quickly, the anger is transferred to your neighbor; you cannot wait to tell him what just happened and how he is responsible for losing the million-dollar deal you have been waiting for so long. Then, you realize that you are in the middle of traffic, so you must act. You consciously start breathing strongly, trying to calm yourself down. Unfortunately, just after, your mind starts thinking about how bad this will look to your boss. Losing the potential deal may mean you won't be promoted, so your mind automatically creates an excuse that sounds more critical than the real story about the neighbor.

On the contrary, the conscious side would have an unlike reaction. Probably a nervous laugh, telling yourself this is not actually happening. On the conscious side, there is a sense of awareness and understanding that the universe does not spin around you and that you cannot control everything. It is almost comical to think about all the variables for that happening: having that specific neighbor, the client being in town that week, deciding to call and schedule the call at a specific time, deciding the meeting to be at 8 am instead of noon, forgetting to fill out the gas tank the day before, the football match, the alarm not being laud enough, etc. You also know that if the deal with the client is profitable for both parties, it will happen regardless of being late for the meeting, and you can find a way for that to happen. You may also think that you are so lucky she did not make it on time or can meet later that day. Finally, you feel confident about the job you have done for months, so this minor issue would not affect your boss's trust. As the conscious side is fearless, when you connect with it, your body knows you are not in danger, so no cortisol or adrenaline is needed to protect you, plus you don´t need to feed the negative thoughts about yourself or the people around you.

Now, be honest with yourself and find out which one of the sides defines you the most and how you react most of the time. However, if you feel you have been on the conscious side most of your life, the "love side", ensure that you have not been forcing yourself to feel good and pretending you are fine, even when you are furious inside. It is not the same. Please ensure you are on the conscious side because you actually know how to be free of negative emotions and thoughts. To confirm this is your case, think about the home you were educated as a child. You were probably raised in an environment where they taught you to cultivate the gift of letting things go easily and focusing on what is important in life. Therefore, you learned to react naturally, strongly and optimistically to difficult situations.

Spirituality, and reaching happiness and joy has nothing to do with not expressing emotions or hiding what you really feel from the outside world. On the contrary, hiding emotions and pretending everything are forms of bypassing. Rather, higher levels of consciousness are related to how you feel inside and your deepest thoughts to decrease pain and unnecessary suffering.

Consciousness is how we perceive the world. It is the builder of our reality. And even when we don't know if consciousness is a biological product or the spirit of human beings, we know how it feels. It is the byproduct of everything we need to navigate life and experience the universe— biology, energy, feelings, thoughts, and senses. Thankfully, as conscious beings, we can transform that consciousness and build our reality and the perceptions of that reality. You can do the necessary work to pass from the fear side to the love side; in other words, raising your level of consciousness about the world, your body, and your intentions. This marks the difference between losing your temper and courageously laughing in life. This is spirituality, the difference between getting upset with the world you are in and trusting life. It is the relationship you decide to have with events unfolding before you.

Life Purpose is in the section because it is one of the paths you use to transform your reality. And as life purpose teachings are not provided to kids in the modern western world —honestly, I don't know about it in the eastern world— it is our responsibility as adults to discover that purpose. Even when many say there is no purpose in life and that we are simply the result of random events of nature, psychological research has proved that having a purpose is essential for our well-being. Don't you think it is better to do the best to have a life with meaning and to pursue our happiness and a legacy for the world than to only work for others so you can pay your bills and by stuff?

Thomas Hora, the recognized Hungary psychiatrist, said: "All problems are psychological, but all solutions are spiritual." This quote means that when the other aspects of life are unbalanced, the only aspect that can bear your life and move out of discomfort is the connection with consciousness, the spiritual aspect, which is the director of your life, the natural fuel, the energy you need to make things change and happen.

Exercise – Qualify Your Equilibrium

Now that you have an idea of other vital aspects of your life, it is time to qualify how fulfilled you feel with each one of the aspects from 1 to 5— where one is low fulfillment and five means high fulfillment.

Close your eyes, take a couple of deep breaths and think about where you stand in every one of those aspects. Write down the first number that appears in your head. Next to each qualification, in a phrase, define an action or whatever you could start doing now to improve it. Do not overthink. We are still halfway through setting your life goals. I want you to create an idea, a perception of what you can do. Write down whatever you think first. Remember to add the profession and career aspects to the list, as others aspects you want to consider.

Life Aspects	Qualification (1-5)	Action to improve
Profession and Career	4 (Example)	Start my own business (Example)
Money		
Immediate Family	...	...
Romantic Relationships	...	...
Adventure and Entertainment	...	...
Surroundings and physical environment		
Body and Health	...	...

Community and Social Life		
Your relationship with nature	...	...
Art and Creativity	...	...
Intellectual and Rational Development		
Spirituality and Purpose	...	...
Others?	...	...

Suppose you feel there are lower levels than your professional and career aspect. In that case, you are likely discovering that your job is not the only reason impeding you from finding joy and peace. Everything is connected inside our minds.

Chapter 7 – Defining Real Success

"Try not to become a man of success, but rather try to become a man of value."

- Albert Einstein -

Like everything else we perceive from our civilization, the meaning of modern success has been created by the *invisible hand* and, and according to the development of our society. In today's world, most people live under pressure to pursue success, and being unsuccessful is an additional fear people must deal with in their lifetime. And even when they fear the obvious, like unemployment and the inability to pay for their children's school, the fear of comparing themselves to others' success is the new biggest fear that my clients discovered when working with me.

This chapter's concepts will put the meaning of success in perspective so that you understand better where success comes from and how you can transform success in your life. Success is the fifth layer of the *Matryoshka Method,* and little by litter, you are getting closer to the core of discovering who and what you are. At the end of the chapter, you will meditate to open your heart and mind to assimilate better what is coming in the next chapter.

A Change in the Meaning of Life

In ancient Greece, finding the meaning of life was the center of our existence. Picture Socrates and Plato walking around Athens, raising the level of consciousness not only of the ancient Greeks but of all the generations to come. A couple of thousand years later came the Middle Ages when the rise of the western world started, and the Catholic Church was the protagonist, believing in the "real" God was the cornerstone of our civilization. Next was the Renaissance period marking a shift from a feudal, religious, and intellectually static society to a more secular, humanistic, and intellectually dynamic one when men were declared the center of the universe. A period that marks the beginning of the modern world and one of the most important periods of our whole history.

The question today is, what is the center of our current civilization? I've tried asking my personal friends this question and discussing the purpose of our existence and how humanism affected our religious and spiritual beliefs. But unfortunately, many are likely to leave the table or change the topic immediately. It felts like something beyond disliking existentialist questions was bothering them, and they were hiding from knowing the answer. Luckily for me, and through my curiosity and eagerness to find my tribe, I've found the people with whom I can discuss these questions with no discomfort.

Hopefully, at this point of the book, you feel better reflecting on this idea because I want you to take some time and imagine the kind of stories historians will talk about us a couple of thousands of years from today. It is not hard to believe that they will say we were a communication-centered civilization. However, to me, communications and its technology refer mostly to the inventions that helped shrank the world and allowed us to accumulate tons of data and information. Still, it is normal to think this is the right answer and that these inventions are the pinnacle of what defines our civilization. If we pay close attention to how we live today, it is like we could only survive with cell phones, the internet, and Wi-Fi. Often the first thing we do in the morning is to check our phones instead of saying good morning to the ones we love. Not a single day passes without being connected to a certain type of machine or device. It is tough not to connect our current civilization to this; sometimes, it feels like we have become slaves of these technologies.

The Anthropocene era is another possible description of how future generations can describe our current civilization. Even though this means 'the era of humans,' it has a connotation that is not as positive as it seems. This label suggests that we have shaped the environment and changed mother earth's natural course: climate change, biodiversity loss, and ocean acidification are just some examples. Thus, it is not abnormal that any people ensure these changes lead to the end of our species. Even when there is no agreement around these topics because others still believe we are on time to recuperate the Earth, we only need to see photographs of the Earth at night; to easily observe, we have massively changed the aspect of our planet from a distance.

Hopefully, in the future, science and technology will help solve the issues humans are causing and prevent cancer so we can live 120 years, have holidays on the moon and go for exchange programs on Mars. It is impossible to deny that science and technology are directly accountable for improving the quality of human lives and opening the door to a new understanding of our species.

However, technology has advanced faster than the collective consciousness of our civilization. It is getting to a point where we are losing the capacity to interact with other human beings. It seems easier to stare at a screen all day than to sit down with our loved ones, look each other in the eyes, have a deep conversation and be present. It is like it is more difficult every day to stand ourselves, our minds or other people's minds. And if it was simpler to observe strangers' stories on social media and television than to go out and create our own stories.

I wonder if a new renaissance period is about to come, a moment in our evolution where there is a rise in our collective consciousness and when finding non-materialistic purposes is the center of our civilization. Hopefully, our civilization is reaching the point where instead of focusing on collecting things and looking for empty entertainment, we focus on becoming better human beings, centered on love and kindness, as we can reconnect to our souls and our essence.

Introducing Mr. Ego

Today, our society is forgetting what we are, leaving others in charge of what is essential for our human existence: psychologists understand better who we are, psychiatrists are in charge of controlling our moods with chemicals, our personal trainer tells us how to move and how many times to do an exercise, and total strangers are the ones watching after our children. As a result, we are losing the capability to manage our lives, which is contradictory in today's world when we have more objective knowledge than before to comprehend what we are made of and what we need as humans. But the answer is not as complicated as it seems: we just let our egos drive our lives.

The concept of the ego you are familiar with may differ from the concept of ego that I will keep using for the rest of this book; therefore, pay close attention to the following scenario and the inquiries around it so we can agree on a similar concept.

Imagine you are alive just after we stopped being nomads and became farmers. Try to use your imagination as much as possible to put things in perspective and visualize how you would feel living in those times without considering that life was better before; life was just different. Imagine, for example, how would it be a society with no technology, electricity, books, school, employment, church, or alcohol. Instead, survival, building strong friendship ties and harmony with neighboring tribes were the main drivers of the community.

Imagine you are a kid living in those times. You are only ten years old and live in a rustic wooden home with your parents and siblings. Your family cultivates wheat and has two cows that provide milk. You live in a small peaceful community near a river and next to other farms.

The community has a single leader. She is the oldest in the community, around 38 years old. Remember, at those times, life expectancy was not as high as today. As a leader, she helps centralize the villagers' decision-making process and is the medicine woman. Everyone respects her; she is believed to be the wisest person alive.

On a normal day, you usually wake up early, before the sun is up, to work the land with your father, and at noon you are free to play around the forest with other kids and fish in the river. However, today is special because the village has a birth ceremony. The day before, the leader had announced to the village that a baby would be born. And as a tradition, all the members will prepare a ceremony and pray for the baby and the mother's life. So instead of working the land, you will collect flowers to make face paints and build costumes with other kids. In addition, mothers and women will sacrifice some of the animals to prepare special meals, and men will build the ceremony stage for fire and dancing. It is a very important ceremony because the probability of that baby and the mother surviving is very low. They believe every village member's commitment is vital to building a magical energetic space for everything to go smoothly.

Everyone is filled with joy and very excited about the birth ceremony. Today will be one of the best days of your early existence; it will be one of the few times you participate in a ceremony like this and see a newborn. You feel like the luckiest kid in the world.

Close your eyes for a moment and travel to this childhood.

Now, imagine what it means to be successful in those times. In a place where few differences existed among the community members. Most people had similar opportunities even when some ranks were established. Consequently, success meant having a father to teach you how to work the land, own a couple of cows, live nearby a river, live for more than 38 years, survive childbirth, and witness a baby's birth.

Nevertheless, when we bring the same scenario into today's world and if today you had a simple life, as the one described, you would be considered in absolute poverty and be an example of unsuccess. Moreover, you would feel very unhappy witnessing other kids go to school, have technology, electricity and cars, and have a longer life expectancy for themselves and their children.

What makes people who lived 5,000 years ago happy but miserable today living under the same conditions is called the ego. The ego is an illusion created by the culture and programmed in your mind that tries to define what or who you are according to the costumes and beliefs created by your environment. It's a concept that builds in your mind when you start being self-conscious and comparing yourself with the rest of what you see and experience growing up. The ego is planted when you are a kid, cultivated when you reach adolescence and young adulthood, and when it is not recognized, harvested for the rest of your life. When ignored or not recognized, like in most people walking on Earth, the ego is the main driver of people's existence. It defines aspects of their personality, makes most of their decisions, defends ideas and beliefs of that environment, and establishes most of their values.

However, the ego is not your whole. It is only a part of your mind continuously blocking the rest of what you have inside; for example, your heart and soul desires. When the ego is the leading master of your life, there are aspects about you you cannot recognize because you hid them years ago and suppressed them in your subconscious mind because the world that surrounded you told you they were wrong or immoral. Today, in your adulthood, that suppression communicates with you through feelings and emotions, most of which you cannot consciously understand, but that your rational mind can only interpret according to that ego's programs.

In conclusion, Mr. Ego, as I will refer to it, is closely linked with the concept of success defined by the culture, which drives your entire life and what you think is valuable for your life and your value as a person. Therefore, understanding this concept and how this is manifested in your life is crucial to answering the questions of what and who you really are and what you want from life moving forward.

What is to be successful today?

Globalization, marketing, consumerism, material possessions and the absolute abundance of the current society have reinforced the concept of modern success. Things we can easily see and touch, or whatever is in the three-dimensional world, mark the difference between success and being a total loser. Success today can be summarized as having a very important job in a millionaire corporation or startup, collecting many things, having extravagant experiences and vacations, and having extra money to pay to stay forever young. Also, we could include having a united family is essential to be considered successful, but in today's world, as we discussed in the previous chapter, that is no longer necessary. Some have decided that being alone is what they want and an apparent option for a successful life.

The concept of success is just a program unconsciously uploaded to your brain by your surroundings. Mr. Ego is the entity within your mind that defends that concept, and it will do anything to defend that status if ever threatened. It is real, part of your reality, and a big portion of your life's paradigms.

However, what Mr. Ego says regarding happiness and personal fulfillment is not necessarily true. Achieving everything that makes someone successful doesn't guarantee happiness or inner peace. As we saw in the previous chapter, we must balance our life to feel satisfied and complete. People who are professionally and financially successful according to current standards, but are still looking for the next thing to feel happy, are good examples of what happens when people ignore the complete spectrum of the human experience.

We all have met people who apparently have it all but still live angry, under continuous anxiety, and depend on external substances like antidepressants and recreational drugs to feel happy. Others who may have it all are ruled by negative emotions such as jealousy, envy, criticizing, blaming and complaining. I hope you agree, but neither of these cases sounds like a good and effective description of real success. On the contrary, we have also met people who aren't professionals and have very few possessions, who have also had tough life experiences, lost someone important and are financially broken but still are genuinely happy and spread joy most of the time. If you observe them closely, they have also cultivated characteristics such as compassion, love, a giving personality and humility.

The main difference between the person who has everything but is unhappy and the person who has just the minimum and is happy is how they embrace life. Without a doubt, the last ones are the ones that have consciously understood something that many other mortals haven't. They have comprehended that happiness depends on the side of the spectrum where they decided to be, the love and conscious side or the side based on fear, the unconscious side. However, as them, anybody can shift the gears of their life and ultimately decide who their life's driver is.

If you are still determining who is driving your life or how to take control of the driver's seat, fasten your seatbelt because, in the next chapter and chapter 11, we will differentiate in more detail whether you are mostly ruled by fear or by love, the moment where real transformation can begin; and how by changing some behaviors, you can start moving from one side to the other.

Exercise – Your Own Meaning of Success

Now that you understand that being successful is something the world told you to do, be, or have, it is time to focus on what success means to yourself. And as you already know your dislikes, fears, and values, and you have a good impression of the balance in your life, your idea of success may include the following.

- You don't want to suffer the dislikes anymore.
- You probably want to confront and overcome your fears.
- You want to live your values more every single day.
- And you have a certain set of goals you want to achieve for different aspects of your life.

After you recall all of this, write down a page describing what success means for you today. Then, highlight patterns, common topics, and themes that appear every time.

Also, remember the beginning of this chapter, when we wondered what stories historians would say about our civilization in the future. And include those thoughts in your meaning of success. What is it that you want future generations to talk about you? Do you want them to tell the story of a very successful and stressed manager of an important corporation that probably won't exist anymore? Or what would be the story you want them to tell your grandchildren about you? These ideas are important not because you care what others think about you but because you are the one who defines your personal story. You are the creator of all the things that have happened and will happen in your life. Therefore, it is fundamental to start visualizing the end of that story and how you will tell your personal story of success.

Finally, summarize all those ideas in a single paragraph of success, consolidating what you want the most in your life. With this exercise, you will finish the fifth layer of the *Matryoshka Method*.

Meditation – The Empty Lake

This meditation aims to prepare your mind to receive new ideas, concepts, insights, and programs, so you can start changing the habits that make you feel unsatisfied. It's time to fasten your seatbelts and prepare for a new journey. If you have never meditated before, only read this paragraph and take some time to close your eyes, take a couple of deep breaths and connect with the visualization described here.

Imagine you open your eyes in the middle of a forest—the forest of your dreams. You are alone in the middle of all kinds of trees, colorful flowers, natural sounds, fresh air and a blue sky. You feel at peace and have a deep, warm emotion within your heart.

Out of a sudden, a particular sound calls your attention. It's like this perfect little sound of water running, like a stream or a waterfall. So, you decide to start walking toward that sound. After a while, you begin to see a lot of animals: raccoons, deer, and birds, as if they were following and observing you. You feel a sense of security, like the animals and the entire forest are there to protect you. The trees and the flowers move to open the path for you to reach that body of water. As you walk, you start getting hot, so it would be refreshing to take a bath and a swim. After walking for a few minutes, some bushes open before you, and you see a lake and a little stream of water pouring into it. However, the lake is not as beautiful as everything around you; it looks turbid and dark. And for some reason, that sense of tranquility vanishes, and you start feeling anxious. Grey clouds start moving toward you as if a storm is coming. The animals along your side run away, and the water inside starts to move. It feels like something is in the lake and wants to come out of it.

In the middle of this fear and mental fug, you see a large chain on the other side of the lake. Something you cannot explain tells you that the chain belongs to a plug that, when pulled, empties the lake and washes away everything that is inside the lake. You know the rain of the dark clouds coming will help fill up the lake again with new and clear waters. So you run to the other side of the lake and pull that chain. It works! The lake's water starts decreasing, emptying the dirt and the imminent threats inside. Soon the space will be ready to receive new water. And you know that clearer water will make you feel at peace again, as is everything around you.

After a few minutes, the rain filled up the lake again, the dark clouds disappeared, and the blue sky came back. Now, you can see the bottom of the lake, and you are ready to jump in the water and let it cleanse your body and mind to return to the warm feelings of peace you had at the begging. Now, you are ready for a little nap.

...

Chapter 8 – Trust Yourself

"Love isn't something we invented. It's observable, powerful, it has to mean something... Maybe it's some evidence, some artifact of higher dimensions that we can't consciously perceive... Love is the one thing we're capable of perceiving that transcends dimensions of time and space. Maybe we should trust that, even if we can't yet understand it."

- Christopher and Jonathan Nolan, Interstellar-

In previous chapters, we developed some ideas about losing our connection with human nature because we are so immersed in what we have been told to become, our ego, that we have forgotten our instincts and intuition. Therefore, this chapter aims to connect to ourselves and our souls and understand who and what we really are. If we don't know what we are or who we are, there is no way to know how we can trust ourselves.

Who and What are You?

We have all heard throughout our lives this familiar question, "Who are you?" and when people reply, the answer normally looks something like this—I'm Claudia, I'm 31 years old, and I've worked for a consulting company since I was 22. These, however, are the answers to questions related to your name, your age, what you do, and for how long.

If you try it again and go deep o answer the question: Who are you?

You may think further and answer— I was born in Mexico, I am an engineer, and my father's name is Pedro. I also went to Mexico School District and moved to Georgia for my diploma. These answers, however, relate to your place of birth, profession, father's name, and the places you went to study.

Even when now, it seems like a tough question, they may not be wrong or right answers. However, I want you to be aware that most of your answers when someone asks who you are, are, in fact, similar to the concept we discussed earlier and the fact that you are the result of your surroundings—The place you were born, the name they the assigned to you, your career, your profession, etc.

But what happens when we modify the question to "What are you?" instead of who. The answer would probably be different and may sound like this—I'm an adult female homo sapiens.

These answers, however, solve the question of what sex you are and what kind of mammal you are, probably not taking us to the true complexity of the answer we may be exploring because we are more than a simple classification of gender and taxonomy.

I cannot answer who and what you are, those questions need to be answered by yourself, but I can help you understand pertinent concepts about the current human perception of <u>who</u> and <u>what</u> we are. "<u>Who you are</u>" is basically an idea, a concept of what your surroundings and culture tell you, and "<u>What you are</u>" is your physical body, what you can see and touch. In other words, it's like people were two separate things: the mind, the idea, and the body.

In addition to these two concepts, there is a third entity to consider when understanding what and who we are. That one "thing" that has always been there— almost impermanent. That "thing" that has witnessed all of your life— from the moment you first started creating the consciousness of self and went to kindergarten to the day you finished middle school and had your first kiss, and that today it is observing how you are a successful professional.

The "thing" is the one aware of your thoughts and feelings. It is the witness of your internal conflicts and self-doubt. It's that "thing" that observes how you express your emotions, that observes you crying when something seems unfair and laughing when things are amusing.

If you recognize it, what do you think it is, "<u>what you are</u>"—your body? Or is this "<u>who you are</u>"—your mind? Is that the brain, or is that the professional?

This thing has had different names during our history and the history of philosophy. In some cultures and religious traditions, that "thing," force, energy, or witness is called spirit (Christianity). In others, Chi and Tao (Taoism), Brahman (Hinduism), or Quantum Self (Imagination Technology). For you to understand better, this entity has remained unchanged throughout your life and will be accompanying you for the rest of that life as if time did not affect it. However, if you compare the two other entities, your mind and physical body have changed. You don't know and think the same things you knew when you were a five-year-old kid, and also, your body has changed immensely since then. Many of the cells you had then are no longer within your brain and body.

You can be free and pick whatever name you want to call that "thing" or entity since every religious tradition and philosopher has defined different names for similar entities. However, if you have declared yourself an atheist, don't believe in life after death, and do not believe in supernatural things, you can pick a less controversial name: the witness, the force, inside energy, or simply consciousness—as I will refer to it for the rest of the book. What is important thing is that you can identify it within you.

This terminology is important to understand the new ideas of the book moving forward. And this is also the best way for me to clarify the concepts we have discussed and their duality: Love vs. Fear, Consciousness vs. Unconscious, and Ego vs.—what do you think that antagonist of the ego is? —the soul.

Even when the soul and the spirit are used interchangeably in some cultures and traditions, I want to differentiate them here. The soul is not a supernatural "force" that will transcend to other dimensions; it is the purest form of your mind and part of your human experience. And when I say mind, I am not necessarily talking about the brain. The brain is like the hardware — that aspect we can see and touch. But when I refer to the mind, it is more about your ideas, programs, concepts, and the essence that was already there when you were born— it would be more like the operative system and the software that runs in the brain and, why not, the body.

Even when the western world is still beginning to understand the mind-body connections, it is essential at this part of the book to start assimilating that that connection is direct. The body cannot live without the mind and vice-versa. And I say beginnings because only 20 years ago, we didn't know that our brain is neuroplastic and can still keep learning new things and changing new behaviors. Most neuroscience discoveries and theories have flourished in the last two decades, and many questions remain to be solved. Nevertheless, some things are not for us to understand, like the fish that swim in the water that cannot understand what water is because it is so surrounded by it.

One of the biggest unknowns is where consciousness is located in the body. After more than 30,000 scientific written papers about consciousness, there still needs to be a consensus about how consciousness emerges or any place of our body that has been identified in which consciousness originates. However, some theories have established a very high relationship between consciousness and the network that connects the brainstem—the portion of the brain that links up with the spinal cord, with the cortex. This conclusion resulted from research by Michael Fox, MD, Ph.D., Assistant Professor of Neurology at Harvard Medical School and Director of the Laboratory for Brain Network Imaging and Modulation.

Others, like the recognized physicist Roger Penrose, and Stuart Hameroff, an Anesthesiologist and Professor at the University of Arizona, have studied the possibility that consciousness is not specifically located in place but arises from the quantum computations in the microtubules of neurons. Similar to this theory, the Australian philosopher David Chalmers has proposed that consciousness may be a fundamental property of the universe, a fundamental feature of the universe, akin to space and time and that it cannot be reduced to purely physical processes of our brain.

Regardless of knowing where consciousness is located, we don't need a scientific theory to prove its existence. Like the fish in the water that does not know what water is, it can feel it in the tides, when it swims and during a storm; you can perceive consciousness and feel what I'm about to explain.

The Ego, Soul and the "Thing"

The following graphic is a basic representation of the relationship among all the mentioned concepts. This depiction seeks to clarify and answer some questions you may have. But you can also feel free to interpret them as you want and according to your beliefs and personal truth. I'm sure you will comprehend because we are made of the same stuff; we are all equals.

	The Thing	
Level of Consciousness	Low	High
Mind	Egoic Mind	Soul
Example of Emotions	Apathy Shame Guilt Anger Fear	Courage Acceptance Joy Love Inner Peace
Life Drivers	Time Driven Rational Judgment	Timelessness Presence Awarness
Attitude Towards Life	Pessimistic Negative	Optimistic Positive

Figure 2 - Picture inspired by the book Power vs. Force by Dr. David R. Hawkins

We all come to this world with the mind in the purest form, body, soul, and spirit, and the consciousness of the self starts emerging in the first years of our lives. When we are growing up, little by little, we absorb and understand the world around us. We got a name by which we respond, learn our family's values and beliefs, and assimilate our country's culture and behaviors. Then, we start being consciously and unconsciously programmed, like a computer, and the environment shapes who we think we are.

As you see in the graphic, as your brain is being uploaded with the programs of our current civilization, your ego starts to form. Gradually, your consciousness or spirit, "the thing," starts moving and focusing on the egoic mind that has been created. With time, Mr. Ego starts taking over, like covering up what was in your mind before, your soul, your essence.

When humans reach adulthood, they forget what they were when they were born and start becoming who they were told to become. The act of forgetting what we are is why the adolescent period of human beings is complex and unexpected. It is like our soul resists strongly being lost and sometimes lost forever. Things do not only happen due to a biological or chemical explanation; the subconscious mind plays a significant role in every moment of our lives. So, next time you face an unbearable teenager, remember that they are saying goodbye to their authenticity and what defines them to become someone "acceptable" for society. Try to be understanding and loving instead of being judgmental.

When the spirit is on the ego side of the spectrum, you tend to be the victim of the world and the victim of the people around you. Regrets from the past and fear of the future basically rule your life and decision-making. When your mind is driven by ego, you tend to suffer more because you live in constant unconsciousness and lack comprehension of yourself and the world itself. What *the invisible hand* created out of you is not really what or who you are. It is an illusion continuously operated by the system, and living in that false reality adds unconscious pain to your mind-body.

We all are plugged into this system, The Matrix, which is not more than the natural product of historical events that converge in a singular space-time—the result of the *invisible hand* acting through time. The Matrix can be visible in the form of buildings, highways, technology, institutions, contracts, art or fashion. But it is also invisible in the form of cultural beliefs, ideologies and mental programs. This Matrix is the main blocker of your consciousness, preventing it from observing the content of your soul. However, this does not mean whether you are good or bad; we all learn values, morality and ethics from our environment and biology. This only means that your real self and nature have been replaced by the materialism of the western world, and your consciousness is mainly focused on those specific programmed ideologies and beliefs.

In figure two (2), you can understand why spiritual growth is also called consciousness expansion. In this process, we increase the consciousness of the self and expand the vision of ourselves and the universe. This new vision allows us to have a different vision of our lives and how to change our reality. If before, we could only see the content of "The Matrix," where apathy, shame, guilt, anger, and fear were the prevailing emotions when we stop being ignorant of who and what we are, a new reality and new truths emerge.

For this reason, spiritual growth is not about being more than others or more intelligent; that would be an ego's attitude. Instead, it is about meeting our authentic selves and connecting to the infinite possibilities outside "The Matrix," a place where you start leaving behind a lower frequency of emotions and meet others such as courage, acceptance, joy, love and inner peace. Consciousness expansion is more about leaving behind the limiting and toxic beliefs that make us suffer and connecting more with the ones that make us feel better about life.

Nowadays, more and more people are only looking for answers to understand their life, especially the pain they have suffered for many years. Similarly, some others are consciously looking to unplug themselves from this Matrix of reality—rebirth, awaken, or find themselves. In both cases, they know there is something else out there that they need to comprehend or something they need to get riff of to find peace and happiness. Looking for these answers takes people to a path of self-knowledge, healing and understanding a new perspective of their realities, which in many cases, they discover to be the source of much of their pain.

All of my clients find me in moments of uncertainty and self-doubt. They feel like they are failing in their professional lives—whether they had a humiliating boss who made their work life miserable, quit a company that didn't offer growth, or were fired without understanding a different reason than not being good enough. Similarly, my transformation to find back my soul started when I was feeling like a failure, as I mentioned in chapter 2. After decades of trying to succeed in a corporate world that I disliked that much and realizing that I would never be "successful."

In all of these cases, it is the ego the one who feels uncomfortable because it is not meeting the expectations of the Matrix. Still, this doesn't make it less of a painful experience. In my case, facing this and discovering that the life and the job I fought for ages made me unhappy has been one of the most painful experiences of my life. Additionally, I could not see at that time that without this pain, I would have never started to understand who I was and what I wanted in life.

Unfortunately, many people will go through their lives letting Mr. Ego rule. Even when they unhappiness or in deep suffering will never be an indication to look for understanding and transcend that reality. This happens because they have always lived the programs and the emotions linked to the Matrix, and they believe there is nothing else to be uncovered. Like the fish in the water, they don't think there is life beyond that reality. Thus, they will never challenge their unhappiness or the cultural programming of their surroundings, and will eternally blain others, the unfairness of life and the Universe.

However, this is not to be judged or blamed. We are all creating different experiences, and everything is acceptable. Some people are more disruptive, curious, nonconformists and rebels than others. Additionally, everyone has a unique path and a purpose, and the lessons and how people learn to grow and transcend in life are always different.

It doesn't matter what your case may be, what point of your personal and spiritual growth path you are embracing now or why you have this book in your hands. What is important is that by reading this book, you connect better with your authentic self and improve your interaction with reality. You have only one life to be you, so it is time to keep looking for the life your soul always wanted.

When you start moving your spirit to a higher level of consciousness, and your spirit moves towards your soul, you begin to discover your real self's truth. Fears tend to fade because most come from the comparisons you make with others and the judgment of society's limiting beliefs. When you start understanding your essence, you also start understanding the essence of others and the universe; therefore, feelings of judgment, guilt, and resentment vanish in front of you. Time, past and future lose importance and meaning because you no longer need to hurry to become something else, in someone they expect. You start observing you are whole, and nothing else is needed to feel complete and joyful. The present moment becomes all you have, and enjoying life is natural to the point that the automatic modes that have driven your daily life for many years start disappearing.

Remember the empty lake meditation? Please keep it empty a little longer for what is coming in the book; we are not in Kansas anymore.

The Point of No Turning Back

Buddhism says that we all have the Buddha nature inside us. In the context of our graphic, it's when the spirit is in connection with the soul, a state of pure consciousness and enlightenment. And even when we may never experience what Buddha or other enlightened characters of our history, like Jesu, did, we can work to decrease our unconscious suffering and replace them with more moments of awe and filled with genuine joy. In other words, a life worth living.

Whatever decisions you are making right now regarding your career and job should be made at a higher level of consciousness, where you can see better what part of yourself to start trusting. Of course, this may not guarantee the expected outcome of a dream come true, but the probability of reaching your definition of success is way higher.

In higher levels of consciousness, you understand that you must empower yourself to achieve what you want and stop expecting or waiting for others to do anything. At the same time, you begin to assume better the consequences of your decisions — more peacefully, without regret or resentment. You will remember every time that life is not unfair or wrong and that life just is what it is.

If you continue making decisions based on your ego, you will never feel fulfilled. You will continue being driven by a concept of success that will never be accurate or aligned with your soul. Living in constant dissatisfaction and disappointment whether or not you achieve the things the world told you you should get. You will be trapped in a never-ending search for something without even knowing what it is, just like a hamster on a wheel.

It is impossible not to be rational or not have an ego. Even the most enlightened people deal with ego. It is part of the design of our mind and the entity we need to operate in this tridimensional. We must rely on our rationality and Mr. Ego to plan things, finish tasks, work with others, and enjoy life's little pleasures. This means that being more in tune with yourself is not about getting rid of your ego but understanding how it operates so you can leave behind the programs pulling you back from a life of peace and joy.

Even when every exercise and philosophy shared in this book aims to help you discover what your soul wants and help you make a better decision, I'm going to share four specific tools to consider and start working on to raise your consciousness, be more present, and be more aware of your real self and your reality. All of them are connected and complement each other, and the more practice one, the others become clearer.

Before we move to the tools, I want to clarify some things:

1. Raising the level of consciousness is not a final goal you will achieve in many years of practice; it can happen now, in one moment of connection with the real self.
2. It is not where you are supposed to go, so then you'll be happy; happiness can be only found in the now, not in the future and not in the past.
3. It is not something that is made to change who you are because you are broken and need to heal something; it is about finding the pieces of yourself hidden under the culture's programming and seeing your authentic self, maybe for the first time in your life.
4. The tools to raise your level of consciousness will help you know yourself better and stop the mechanical and automatic lives you have been designed to live. There are ways to stop time and find a place without worries to be at peace within yourself and the universe.

The following tools can be implemented in your life at any moment or in any order. However, you can start implementing them in the order I describe here, introducing a new tool every week or every other week. In this way, within one to two months, you have completely integrated them into your system.

Tool #1 – Meditation

You have probably heard before this book the benefits of the practice of meditation. It has been a trend in the last decade; people discuss this topic more and more in the workplace. However, some people might have told you that meditating is complicated or could be especially complicated because you are always overthinking. Others have probably said that it doesn't work for everybody and only for a few. And others may have told you that meditation is practicing a religion or probably something related to a cult. Regardless of what you have heard or experienced with meditation, please erase all your thoughts about it, and let's explore it with a fresh start. Everyone has a unique and personal experience with meditation; what I have experienced and discovered while meditating is certainly different from what you will discover. Additionally, experiencing meditation is not only you do one or three times; you should try it and be consistent before judging it.

Before we get to the practice of meditation, and especially for those who don't care so much about the metaphysical side of discovering who you are, I want to explain the science behind meditation. Thousands of recent scientific studies have proven that the brain's capacity improves after meditation for a few weeks. This discovery goes in line with the neuroplasticity ability that had been already discovered in which they confirmed the brain could change, expand and create new neural pathways, which was believed to be impossible after reaching adulthood. In other words, this means we can enhance our brain's responses through training like we do to train our muscles.

In one particular study performed on a frequent mindfulness meditator, researchers compared their brains with a control group of non-meditators. After measuring the brains, they noticed that, on average, frequent meditators have a thicker frontal cortex and thinner anterior insula. The first is related to attention, and the second is related to stress and anxiety.

Some people may argue that those differences in the brain make people meditate and not the opposite, so meditation could not be the cause of changes in the brain. However, to counteract this theory, studies have also been performed on non-meditators showing changes in the brain and their behavior after a few weeks of meditation. Other people have also argued that meditation has nothing special because any new activity or mental training, such as learning a language, also changes the brain. However, meditation has the particularity of transforming brain parts related to controlling emotions and awareness.

Finally, and to close the scientific session around meditation, I want to share with you one of the studies performed by Dr. Richard Davidson, a recognized neuroscientist at the University of Wisconsin. In the early 2000s, by direct request of his holiness, the Dalai Lama, Dr. Davidson, performed studies on meditation and experiments on Buddhist monks. The results were extraordinary. They flew some monks from Nepal and India to Wisconsin to scan their brains using EEG (electroencephalography) and functional magnetic resonance imaging (fMRI) to understand the brains' behavior while meditative. On average, the monks in the study had more than 30,000 hours of meditation, which is like eight hours of daily meditation over ten years. It is believed that this was one of the first times in the history of neurology that they put electrodes in such professional meditators. What they found, at first, was so unusual that they thought the equipment was broken and needed to be fixed before moving forward; they found that the gamma-oscillations in their brains lasted seconds when practicing compassion meditation. For a point of reference, non-mediation gamma-oscillations last only a few milliseconds, thousands of times more than the average they ever measured.

Gamma oscillations refer to neural oscillations, which are a prominent feature of the brain's electrical activity and are among the highest-frequency oscillations in the brain, typically ranging from 30-100 Hz; while others, like alpha oscillations, occur in the range of 8-12 Hz, beta in the range of 12-30 Hz, theta in the range of 4-8 Hz, and delta in the range of 1-4 Hz. Gamma waves have been associated with conscious processing, such as perception, attention, memory formation and retrieval and emotional regulation, suggesting that long-term meditation practice may lead to changes in brain activities that benefit these brain characteristics.

There are still many questions to be answered and much research to be done to understand better how the brain process meditation. Still, there are many proofs of the benefits of meditation, such as raising our consciousness and attention and increasing the positive states in our brains. And even when I can keep listing these benefits, starting meditation is a decision you must make from your heart. To do so, you must stop listening to the excuses and limiting beliefs our culture, Mr. Ego and bad habits tell you.

I had my first experience with meditation in my early 20s, 20 years ago. I have practiced different types of meditation: guided meditation, Transcendental Meditation, and vipassana meditation. In addition, I have been taught Tibetan Buddhist meditation, participated in meditation and mindfulness courses, spent more than four hours meditation without stopping for several days in a row, and read plenty of books about the topic. However, people don't have to do everything I did to become good and constant meditators. You neither need to follow a new religion or school of thought.

The following meditation techniques aim to embrace your thoughts differently, trying not to engage with them or the feelings and thoughts they may produce, cultivating awareness of the present moment— the now. I'm unsure if Buddhist monks or the Dalai Lama can completely silence their thoughts. Even so, it does not matter because that is not your ultimate goal when practicing meditation for the first time, and it won't be for many other years in the future.

Stage 1 – Posture: Some people like to sit on the floor or a cushion, crossing their legs or in a lotus position, but you don't need to be in a difficult or painful position to be able to meditate. On the contrary, this may be counterproductive because your mind will focus on the discomfort. So instead, you can sit in a chair with your feet on the floor and back straight, avoiding lying against the backrest. The straight back is very important because that will keep you awake and attentive. After you feel comfortable, please close your eyes softly. You don't need to push it. Finally, gently set the tongue over the palate, like a caress, and stay as still as possible.

Stage 2 – Breathing: In chapter 6, we discussed the human body having 11 different systems and more than three trillion cells working for you in a single second. Well, out of all our body's systems, the one we can easily manipulate as easily as we can control our thoughts is the respiratory system. Breath can be held, accelerated, and controlled just by the mere act of thinking about it. We can send a signal to the system, and that's done. Just try it now and take a deep breath. Easy.

Before you engage in meditation, being aware of your breathing is essential. Breathing works like a VIP ticket to your inner peace. I recommend doing three things: First, be aware of the air entering through your nose and your lungs; be aware of the temperature, when your breath in is always colder than when you exhale; feel the movement of your chest and your belly; notice that when you breathe deeper, your belly will expand wider. Second, take three deep breaths before starting to breathe naturally. Finally, start counting each inhalation and each exhalation. For example, Inhale 1, exhale 2, inhale 3, exhale 4... until 27. When you finish the cycle, start over again. You can start over again when you get lost in the count because your thoughts will drive you out of it. Try it. If 27 sounds like a high number because you never make it to it, you can start experimenting with the number 12, for example.

Stage 3 – Observing: Getting lost in your thoughts while counting and starting over is also part of meditation, so don't get frustrated. Observe, and go back several times until you are at least making 3 or 4 cycles. However, make sure you are aware of your thoughts when they appear, observe the thought and then let them go. Observe them with the idea of realizing the nature of the thoughts and how they come and go from your mind. But try not to engage your feelings or judge that thought; let it pass through your mind. If new thoughts and feelings arise, do the same, observe them, be aware of them, let them pass and go back to counting your breath. Congratulation, you are already meditating.

There is a frequent metaphor used by meditation teachers when they describe the mind in a meditative state. Imagine that the purest state of mind, the soul, is like a blue sky, and our thoughts are the grey or white clouds that cover it. It is hard to see the blue sky in our minds because our brains are usually full of thoughts, ideas, judgments, and worries. But gradually, when you include meditation in your daily life, clouds will dissolve faster, and the sky will be bluer and easy to observe. Little thoughts will always appear, but never again so powerful to cover the entire sky.

Stage 4 – The Third Eye: After counting your breathing and observing your thoughts, the next meditation stage is paying attention to the sixth chakra or the third eye. This part of the body is the name given by the space in your forehead between your eyes by some eastern traditions. Remember, you don't need to believe in dharmic traditions like Hinduism to practice meditation; I am just sharing some meditation techniques and familiarizing you with the language. Also, this section in our head is close to the prefrontal cortex at the front of the brain, typically associated with attention and awareness. Stay there as long as you want and observe. Observe everything that unfolds in your mind and feelings. Observe everything that distracts you from your surroundings. Observe your body and what comes from within. But do not engage in particular thoughts, feeling or sensations; always return with your eyes closed to the attention to your forehead.

The first time, second, third and fourth time you do this, you may need help finding a reason to practice meditation, and soon you will again believe it is boring and stop trying. However, you will feel more comfortable, calm, and at peace with the practice after the sixth or seventh time. Trust me! Especially because I'm not an expert meditator like the Buddhist monks who have hundreds of thousands of hours of meditating and were born in it. I had to discover meditation against a culture that rejects and cannot understand meditation.

You can also use guided meditations or Yoga Nidra; most people start this way. However, other ways are available, especially when you want to practice more profound meditation. To reach the inner space where the answers to the deepest question will be solved, you have to learn how to meditate with your mental space only and not by using external voices. Yes, you can experiment with everything called meditation; please do it. Say yes to meditation applications and classes, especially because meditating with others is very powerful. As I said at the beginning of this section, everyone has a different experience with meditation, but always remember that the only thing you need to meditate is you and your presence.

Stage 5 – Scan your body: Another alternative you can use, instead of focusing on the third chakra or as a complement, is to scan your body. From the bottom of your body, your feet, to the top of your head, move your attention to every part of your physical body, external and internal:

1. Start with the right foot and the right leg. Then move to the left foot and the left leg.
2. Move to the front of your trunk, through your belly and chest.

3. Then move your attention to your lower back and the spine to the upper back.
4. Continue with the right hand and arm to the left hand and the arm.
5. Finally, go to the neck and throat until you reach your face and scalp.

Do it as slowly as possible, and with time try to reduce the area you are focusing your attention. For example, in the first days, you can take your attention to the entire foot, then move the attention to your fingers and then to areas of a square inch. Then, like the counting breathing cycles, do the body scans several times and use the same order for that particular meditation. You can also try, for different sessions, going to the inner body, which means what we have under the skin. Muscles, bones, organs and fascia also belong to your body, and focusing on them will take you to deeper states of meditation.

Stage 6 Sustain - Do it daily: eight, 15, 20 minutes... whatever you have available in your day and every day. Meditating early in the morning is better because it is quieter and because it is the first thing you do; your thoughts and worries have not yet invaded your mind, and the practice will flow smoothly. However, remember the more you meditate, the more time you give to yourself for other tasks. Since concentration levels increase when practicing meditation daily, your relationship with time changes and more things will start to be done.

The meditation technique I just shared with you was not a self-discovery. It combines what I have practiced and what has helped me the most. There are other ways or techniques you can use, and as I mentioned before, there are applications you can install on your mobile device to start a meditation practice at home. Whatever works for you is welcome, especially in the starting stages.

The final overall recommendation when meditating is not to be judgmental of yourself. Like most things, a complex task can become simple with time. For example, it was probably traumatic when you first learned to tie your shoes, but after dozens of repetitions, tying them was easy and natural. Try to see meditation as learning something new as a kid—it does not have to be perfect immediately. Plus, you don't need to give it much thought; you only need to sit down and do it. Give it a try; I assure you; you won't lose anything.

Tool #2 - Yoga

I won't spend much time talking about yoga because yoga is about practicing. Plus, it would be best if you practiced with a teacher to ensure you would not harm your body. So instead, I want to give you my point of view and how practicing yoga was one of the most wonderful experiences of my transformation and the transformation I see in my clients.

Yoga has many interpretations, and the story of its origin variates according to the branch of yoga you learn it from. However, as I mentioned, you don't need to follow any school of thought or religion to practice and experience its benefits. For example, some people believe that yoga was invented for men so they can connect to their intuition and the power women already know. Others say that yoga was invented to prepare the body to stay in the lotus sitting position for longer meditations, allowing a more efficient transfer of inner energy.

The word yoga itself means union, which also brings several interpretations—for example, the union of the body, the mind, and the spirit. It is as if it supports the connection and integration of all the parts that make the self. Proper yoga practices bring you to the present moment and help you connect with everything you are, making you forget about the problems you think you have — working like a thought eraser.

However, yoga is not an exercise or an Olympic sport. Yoga is not for athleticism, and yoga is not a competition. And even when practicing yoga can help your flexibility and strength, it is not its main goal. For example, I've practiced yoga for five years, and I still cannot do many inversions or complex postures, nor am I looking to do so as my goal. My practice is based on basic postures that almost everyone with average health conditions can do. Yoga should be better considered as a present for yourself, a tool to balance the energy of your days and your life in the long run. It is more like a prayer of thankfulness for our lives, our bodies, and our mind, and to recognize the good intentions with have in our lives and the life of others.

If you have tried yoga at the gym or done naked, aerial, beer, wine, goat, or power yoga, erase what you know about yoga, and please start over. Look for a studio or a more authentic yogi teacher who is not based only on the teaching of the body or asanas but also on the teachings of the mind and the spirit. If you have tried yoga once, twice, or thrice and still don't like it, try it again by finding a new teacher or school. If necessary, multiple teachers until your energy and the teaching's energy match up. Please do not give up on trying; yoga is not for a few but for everybody.

Mindfulness and meditation are also part of the yoga practice; some teachers open the classes with breathing techniques, as we saw in the previous paragraphs and close the classes with meditation. If you become passionate about you can always include meditation after the yoga session. In this case, you can skip the breathing counting technique and go straight to the third eye and the body scan. You will notice that after yoga can reach a meditative state easier and stay longer.

If you work out, do aerobic exercises, or lift weights, please practice this before yoga and meditation. It is not mandatory since we all have different bodies and can design different routines. But the energy will flow better in your system when you consciously take your body to relaxation after putting it under stress.

Tool #3 – Paying Attention to Your Thoughts

After practicing meditation and yoga for at least a month, it is the best moment to start exploring your thoughts. But, even when you can explore them now, meditation and yoga will bring a lighter perspective on thoughts and a healthier relationship with them.

The first explanation consists of something magical to me and a breakpoint in my transformation. And it is the thought about wondering where the thoughts originate and how they suddenly appear in your consciousness. So, try to think about something other than the neuroscience behind them or how your thoughts are filed and organized in the brain and explore them more according to your personal experience with them.

Thoughts, for example, appear in your brain in two different ways. The first is unconsciously and spontaneously coming from a place inside your mind. The second is when you consciously decide to think about something or due to external stimulation. The unconscious is the involuntary way thoughts appear in your mind every minute, even more frequently, since some researchers have concluded that, on average, a person can have more than 40,000 thoughts a day. The conscious or external way of thought is when we decide what we want to think or because an external source or phenomenon triggers the thought. For example, if I told you, "Think about a pink dolphin now!" you will suddenly think about it and be capable of picturing the dolphin jumping out of the water. By the way, if you didn't know, there are pink dolphins in the Amazon River. Please go ahead and Google it and return to the book because it will be part of the second exploration around thoughts. Even if you have seen pink dolphins before, I want you to have a new image of them in your brain before moving to the next paragraphs.

Continuing with exploring our relationship with thoughts, observe what happened after you saw the dolphin picture. With a very accurate guess, I know that your first reaction was a certain judgment. For example, you might have thought they were adorable or maybe that it was not as pretty as the other dolphins. You might have also observed that they are not completely pink; they are mostly grey, and the shape is less appealing than normal dolphins.

After the judgment happens, something else appears in your consciousness. Something that you may not notice before, and it is not another thought or judgment: it is a feeling, a sensation. So, for example, you might have felt disappointed if you thought the dolphin was ugly or contentment if your expectations were satisfied and you fell in love with their appearance. Accordingly, thoughts are usually accompanied by other thoughts, such as judgments. And these judgments, at the same time, are accompanied by feelings or emotions.

In our daily lives, people normally judge and have a feeling for every single thought their witness in their consciousness. To prove this is true, let's move to deeper thoughts and think about a possible scenario for your future. Let's imagine that you quit your current job, if you haven't already, and imagine that whatever is coming next is going to be worse—you will be paid less salary, your boss is the combination of the worst of all the bosses you've had, you will be working 80 hours per week, and you won't enjoy what you are going to be doing, it's tedious. How do you feel about this scenario? It doesn't feel good.

Even when this sounds very pessimistic, many people make decisions thinking the worst is about to happen. I see this with my clients all of the time. They use this pessimistic practice to reconfirm that their present reality is not bad or can be worse, so they have the perfect excuse for not moving. However, this practice can be positive only like a conscious exercise to observe the thoughts and feelings that flourish as a self-knowledge tool, but never as a decision-making tool. Plus, these people disregard the power of thoughts and intentionally call for those pessimistic scenarios to happen.

Similarly, some of my coachees or clients have told me they do not like to think about brighter futures because they do not want to feel disappointed if things don't happen as they thought. If this also happens to you, please try to stop that practice immediately. Choosing this way of thinking is like preferring to have a mediocre life instead of having dreams and goals in the future, which may be related to hidden subconscious beliefs of lack of self-love, worthiness and self-trust.

Isn't it better to embrace life, knowing that whatever is coming is better and live with a sense of hope? Isn't it better to know that you are closer to your dreams coming true every day? Realize that the fear of not accomplishing your dreams is exactly why you are giving up your dreams and desires before trying.

Not dreaming about a brighter future and the pessimistic strategy can be a double-edged sword if you don't know how to use it, and you may be attracting the opposite of what you want just by denying the power of your mind. We don't know what will happen and how life will unfold tomorrow, but I can assure you that if you don't believe that better things are coming from the bottom of your heart, they won't. If you don't believe you can make it happen and don't believe in yourself, things will be less likely to happen.

The idea of the "paying-attention tool" is not to change your thoughts automatically so you overshadow your real feelings and suddenly become a positive human being. The first goal of the tool is to learn how to carefully observe what you are thinking at the moment thoughts appear to understand their behavior and how the upcoming feeling affects you. The idea is to learn about yourself by carefully observing the thoughts without judging them and observing the feelings rising after the thought without scaping. Then, after acknowledging your current mental situation, your challenge is to step back to avoid the attachment to the sensations and learn about yourself by listening to what your thoughts and feelings have to tell you about actual fears, desires, limiting beliefs and the unconscious program before you change it. As no one can avoid negative or positive thoughts and feelings, embracing and learning from them is one of the first steps toward transformation.

When you get attached to thoughts and feelings that don't bring anything positive to your life and take you to low frequencies, you are playing the games of your egoic mind. By now, you understand that you are not your thoughts. Your thoughts are just bubbles of ideas, impressions, and judgments that come and go to your conscious mind, transmitting energy to your system through feelings and perceptions, whether internally or externally generated. They are manifestations of the programs uploaded to your brain for years, which are not always positive and often very toxic. Toxic programs are harmful because they pull you back from acting toward your goals and the life you deserve and, in the long run, may affect your well-being, mental health and overall life harmony. The good news is that getting rid of them is not as hard as it seems. The first step is being aware of them, understanding what they have to say, and making peace with their toxicity before you start changing them.

Tool #4 – Changing Your Self-talk

To give an example of how harmful a thought can be, think about one time you criticized yourself and some of the words you used. For example, remember a day you thought you were not good enough and told yourself that you didn't have the capabilities to do or change something. Recall the moments you repeatedly remind yourself you did something wrong. For example, when you decided to start a new relationship with someone that was not worthy, sell something you didn't want to trade, move to a new city that didn't welcome you or accept a job you disliked. Or think about simpler things, for example, what you constantly say about your body and face when you look in the mirror. Would you use some of the following phrases to criticize yourself to encourage your best friend?

- "Of course, you cannot do it, you have never been good at it, and you will never do it?"
- "Yup, you screw it up again. You are so stupid; that is what you obviously deserve.
- "You only make wrong decisions; please learn something and stop being so lost. "
- "Look at you; how much weight have you gained? Are you eating a lot of crap? Plus, that does not combine with the wrinkles on your forehead."

And even when this sounds strong, I am not exaggerating. I was this person. I used to criticize myself about everything. I could 't see how harmful this was because, in our society, we believe it is harmless since we often say things about ourselves jokingly. But it is surprising how common this is, and you soon will start noticing if it is your case as well, or surely you will see how others to themselves as if they were their worst enemies.

People should be more aware of their conversations with themselves because this directly reflects their inner thoughts, mental programs and limiting beliefs. Especially if you believe it is not that big a deal because you are just kidding; you are disregarding the power of your thoughts and the words you repeatedly speak toward yourself. If something, those thoughts, the words you say to yourself are the starting point for self-knowledge and self-love cultivation. The underlying messages of those inner conversations are doors to enter your subconscious mind.

Knowing that your negative self-talk usually comes from people around you is important. People from your life today or those around you during childhood formed your operative system's core values and beliefs. And some of these people may not have a positive opinion about life or may not understand the effects of what they are discussing. For example, I always feel like I should sing; I feel passionate about music, which would have been something I could have explored in my life. However, I had never tried it, and I found probably, one of the reasons. When I was six years old, Cecilia, the primary school music teacher, told me I didn't have a good voice and would never sing. Nevertheless, later I learned that one of the most important things for learning to sing is to train your voice, learn the techniques and practice, like everything else you want to do on this planet. However, the voice of someone I thought was the authority at the time could easily have broken a six-year-old's dream. I may not have the voice, but that irresponsible external voice ruined the possibility of trying. Nowadays, I only sing when I do Karaoke with friends. However, I sing only one song, I feel still embarrassed and frightened.

This example was a childish dream that may not have caused a big trauma. However, try to extrapolate this situation to thousands of children around the globe that are constantly told they are bad at something, especially in schools, where very soon in our lives, we start to be compared to others and put into boxes good or bad at something. If something in the school system is the foundation of the toxicity, we will deal with the rest of our lives.

Try to recall something you are not good at or want to do but are too scared of because you may fail, like a new job or profession. And start realizing that if you are blocked from doing any of those new things, you need to improve your conversations with yourself. Let's examine if the following statements may sound like you:

- "I don't have time to find another job,"
- "I am too old to start a new career,"
- "Nobody is going to pay me more of what I make today,"
- "I cannot make money out of something I feel passionate about,"
- "I only have experience doing this,"
- "What if I don't like what is coming?"
- "There are already too many people doing that same thing,"

- "I am not as good as the rest."

I am sure some of these phrases have been part of your mental space. But, even when those thoughts may be supported by valid arguments; usually, the rationale you put behind stopping your dreams and desires are mere excuses to maintain the comfort zone you are so attached to untouched. You have not found a better job or changed your career just because you think all these ideas are true The day you begin changing those simple conversations with yourself into something that sounds more empowering, you will start changing your actions and the intimate relationship you have with yourself. What if your inner voices sounded more like:

- "I will find something way better than what I have today,"
- "I love myself and my family; we all deserve to be happy with what I do,"
- "There world is a space of infinite possibilities; I just need to find the time to look for them,"
- "Of course, I can become an expert on this topic that I love so much,"
- "If enough people were doing this, the problems I see in the world wouldn't exist; of course, there is room for me," or
- "Since and very good at all these things, I am sure I can also be good at many other things and be paid for it."

Finally, remember that most negative self-talk is taught to you by someone specific in your past or cultural belief, as my kinder teacher. I have another example, regarding one of the individuals I worked with who was diagnosed with Attention Deficit Hyperactivity Disorder (ADHD) when he was a kid. According to him, this mental condition is the reason he doesn't read books. He says he cannot concentrate and gets distracted very easily.

However, after months of working together, I realized he has an extraordinary ability to stay still, listen carefully and engage in meaningful conversation. He is very focused and oriented to complete the tasks he intends for the day or the week with no issues. Additionally, he is a very talented musician who loves to spend hours practicing his instrument. I'm not a psychologist or a psychiatrist, but this does not sound like someone with an attention problem. Even though many years have passed since his diagnosis, he still believes he is mentally sick. He constantly reminds himself how incapable he is of doing certain things, even when we have proven they were only ideas and thoughts, not his reality. He simply decided to keep these limiting beliefs in his mind because self-acceptance, encouragement and change are more difficult than doing nothing.

Thus, the next time you think negatively about yourself or your belief is limiting or stopping you from acting, and try to visualize where that idea was planted for the first time. Connecting to that moment is essential to realize that those ideas are not necessarily true, and you must start cultivating new ones. Those ideas are not true because many external voices don't come from a teacher o doctors who might have been mistaken, as in the examples I shared. However, most of the ideas we have from ourselves have come from the closest people who were, for sure, biased, such as our brothers, sister, parents, and friends. Also, consider that some negative self-talk may come from the mainstream media and the movies that make us compare ourselves with celebrities or people who have nothing to do with us.

Now that you are aware this, commit, pay attention to the negative self-talk and start the amazing path of eradicating the limiting beliefs of inferiority and lack of capability in your life.

Our Intuition

The four tools we looked through— meditation, yoga, paying attention to your thoughts and changing your self-talk — aim to increase the levels of consciousness about you and the life unfolding in front of you. When you start practicing these tools, you start perceiving new emotions, sensations, and your relationship with them and the world around you. What starts happening is that, for the first time, you begin listening to voices within you that you have never before or stopped listening to decades ago. New doors of consciousness start to open, and you start visiting places in your psyche you didn't know existed.

One of the voices you will start listening to is the voice of your intuition, which I prefer to call the language of your soul. Even when you have heard this concept before and already have a specific understanding of what it means, you will start changing your relationship with it. This concept will stop being just a gut feeling or the sense of something and will start transforming into a new language.

Understanding your intuition is important because even when you believe you are a rational person who needs to analyze all the variables when deciding instead of listening to your guts, this is not completely true. Your intuition also plays an important role and is the one who decides before your rational mind notices it. So for example, when buying a new house, you would use your rationality to analyze the variables. You may create a table comparing five houses by price, neighborhood, size, and features. After gathering the data, house number one has the best qualifications: all you expected for a house you always dreamed of having. But for some reason, you pick and buy number four, the house that did not have any of the characteristics you had defined before. House number four, for some reason, feels safer and prettier and makes you feel good, even when the features are not what you have defined. This type of unexpected result is how intuition works — knowing without knowing the reasons and not considering the quantitative analysis performed by your rational mind. In this case, your soul was the voice that picked up what was best for you.

Yet, people often don't decide according to their intuition and completely disregard their gut feelings. Instead, they ignore it or believe feelings are less important than numbers and rational analysis. However, intuition helps us consider hundreds of variables we cannot rationalize or transform into numbers. And when we don't listen to our intuition and understand its language, it takes us to places, situations, and events we dislike. Ignoring our intuition is also why we end up in jobs and careers that make us feel miserable and trapped.

The previous statement does not mean you should only follow what your heart and soul tell you and stop using your analytical mind. This statement only means tunning with your inner voices and paying attention to them is important. So that you can differentiate between what from the constant bombard of feelings and contradictions is coming from your intuition and what is coming from your ego — the love side vs. the fear side. But only through the practice of the tools we study in this chapter will the language of your soul become clearer and clearer for you to find the answers you are seeking.

Remember that the soul doesn't know fear, anger, jealousy, shame, or guilt. Instead, the soul is courageous, loving, joyful, and compassionate; meaning means that the more peace you feel with a decision, the more you are listening to the truth of your intuition. I'm not saying that if you are scared, you should not take a certain path; fear will always be a factor in your ego, playing against your deepest desires. This means that the more you know yourself, even when your ego scares you, the easier it will be to choose the best path for your soul. Sometimes, you will even notice why the scariest path is right.

Raising your levels of consciousness will help you connect with your intuition, your purest self, and who or what you are, aside from what your surroundings, the invisible hand, and your ego told you to be once. It is one of the first steps to discovering your truth and blocking the external noise that may aggravate whatever negative feelings you are experiencing. This new connection is the key to listening to your deepest fears and dreams and embarking on a journey to find inner peace and what makes you happy.

Exercise - The Conversations You Have with Yourself

The exercise here is to start meditation and practicing yoga every day for at least two weeks; you can use whatever technique you want and even an application on your phone. You can practice yoga and meditation for 8 to 60 minutes, less time than the one you spend reading tragic news or scrolling on social media, which brings nothing positive to your energetic field.

After two weeks of yoga and meditation, you will also observe your thoughts and start identifying the little lies or negative conversations you are having with yourself. These limiting beliefs impede you from having a good score for each one of the aspects of your life, or at least feeling balanced or complete in most aspects of your life— refer to the exercise in chapter six.

You can write down all the limiting beliefs of negative self-talk you identify during those two weeks or identify them and write them after the two weeks of meditation. Then, draw a line down in the middle of a piece of paper, dividing it into two parallel parts. On the left side, you will write down 2 to 4 negative thoughts or conversations you have with yourself for each aspect of your life —money, immediate family, romantic relationships, adventure or entertainment, etc. Then, on the right side, you will write a new thought again but in a positive and true form.

For example, if the negative thought on the left side sounds like, "I will never find a better job," the positive thought on the right can be: "I will soon find a job I feel happy and passionate about." The positive statement cannot have negative contexts or negation such as 'cannot,' 'impossible,' 'hard,' or 'difficult.' Ensure that a certain part of you know the new thought is true; you cannot trick yourself. Try to find the true tone from your intuition—the voice of encouragement, love, joyfulness, and compassion you expect from your soul.

In the professional aspect, remember the checklists that firms or companies you worked for have used to evaluate whether you are good for the job or ready for a promotion. You may probably know what they "think" you need to improve to be good enough for the promotion. Put those improvement opportunities and negative thoughts on the left side of the paper, and create a new positive set of thoughts for each one. This exercise is to start building self-confidence and trusting what you can do before selling yourself within your company, the next interview, and, why not, your next clients.

At the end of the exercise, consciously cross out each one of the negative thoughts and conversations until you can no longer read them and leave the positive phrases only. Keep the list in a place where you can read it frequently. I recommend reading the new affirmations every day and repeating them aloud from 5 to 10 times each. These new thoughts are designed specifically for you and by you are conscious affirmations, which have more power than generic affirmations that don't speak to your inner fear and desires. Finally, start preparing for what is coming into your life; you are reprogramming your brain, and the changes are imminent.

Chapter 9 – Purpose and Passion

"We don't read and write poetry because it's cute. We read and write poetry because we are members of the human race. And the human race is filled with passion. And medicine, law, business, engineering, these are noble pursuits and necessary to sustain life. But poetry, beauty, romance, love, these are what we stay alive for."

- Nancy H. Kleinbaum, Dead Poets Society -

You have probably heard about the concepts of purpose and passion, but if they don't mean anything to you, don't worry, I will clarify them before we move forward because you will try to identify your purpose and reconnect with your passions. I say "try" because the first time you connect to these concepts may feel strange and fogy. However, with time you will be more in tune with the voices of your real self, and what you feel your purpose is and your passions will become clearer. This attempt to reconnect with both may be one of many tries you will make during your reinvention process. And you can come back to these paragraphs any time you need.

These two concepts are the cornerstones of the rest of the book. They are the heart of the second section of the *Matryoshka Method*, the basis on which you will reinvent yourself. The tools and the method I share with you can help you identify what you feel passionate about and your life purpose. But the most important ones to start the process are the ones we mentioned in the previous chapter: Meditation, Yoga, Paying Attention to Your Thoughts and Changing Your Self-talk.

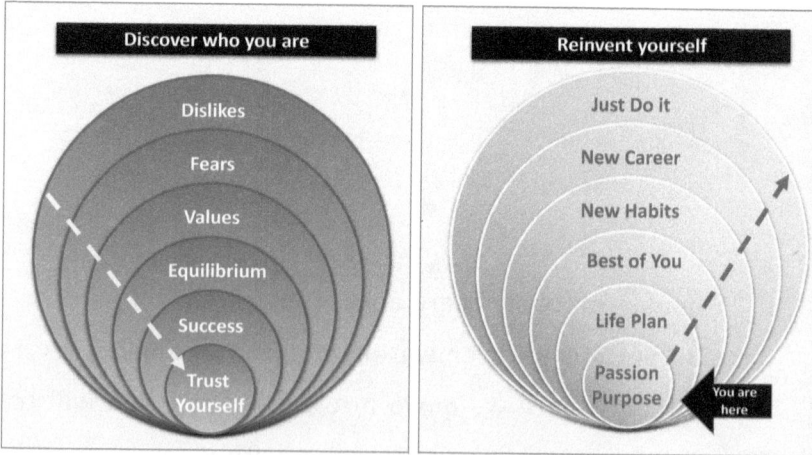

Figure 3 - Matryoshka Method, You Are Here.

Purpose, in general, is the reason for something or the reason people do certain things, the why. In this book, anyway, please consider purpose as the reason behind your life or existence.

Purpose is not specific goals to complete in a certain time. It is not a list of desires to satisfy your ego or a checklist you must complete to go to heaven. Neither is it saving the world and fighting for what is politically correct or a magical destiny you need to pursue during your lifetime.

Your life purpose is an inner power that encourages us to face life— a limitless, timeless power with no excuses. It is the reason to live your life, which makes us fall in love with life itself every day and will do for every moment till the last breath.

Passion, on the other hand, is an intense enjoyment and enthusiasm while doing something. It is what you feel when you think about something or do something you love. It is the foundation of moments of happiness and joy. It is characterized because time losses importance when you do it, and you don't have to think too much to do it – like it easily flows. Passion, however, is not necessarily linked to what you are good at but what you love to do the most; it could but is not mandatory.

Purpose and passion are linked in many ways. However, the most important is that purpose basically is "the why," and passion is "the how." Additionally, the passion for what you do expands infinitely when there is a purpose that really moves. To explore this idea better, I am going to give you a hypothetical example. Suppose you love making cookies- it is your passion: you constantly research the art of baking cookies, you know how to make many types, and you make cookies every day to be sold by the coffee shop in the corner. But, one day, an NGO approaches to you and asks you to make Christmas cookies for poor kids. Your passion now has a bigger purpose, a reason behind it. The purpose, the why, is to make a kid happy at Christmas, and the how is to do what you love the most, baking cookies.

Talking about a life purpose sounds religious to many. However, finding or creating your purpose is not about faith or destiny, like it was a written prophecy you must fulfill during your lifetime. Your purpose is more like a personal declaration that gives you a reason to live. It's the motive you feel you wake up every morning, what keeps your heart beating and will, regardless of what happens in the external world. It is something unique that belongs to you, and no one can take it from you.

When I've asked my potential clients and current clients what their purpose is, I usually receive two types of answers: one is "I don't know." The other is "my family, my wife and kids"—normal answers in a society that doesn't discuss life purpose and confuses purpose and value with making money. But, for example, if you think a little further, asking someone what you do in life is more related to what you do to make money than why you are doing it, how you are changing the world or what you do that makes you happy. For this reason, you are not broken or lost when you don't have an answer or believe that the people you love are your purpose. But if we think a little deeper and imagine a scenario where suddenly your family is not there anymore—say your children moved abroad or you get divorced— what would make you leave your bed in the morning? Does your life make sense in this scenario? Or would you need to find another reason to live, like an excuse?

I want you to understand here that your life purpose does not depend on the circumstances that will change tomorrow, and it does not depend on other people's lives or the decisions they make. It is a statement that comes from your essence, and all of the instances in your life converge— your past, present and future.

Similarly, passion is not something romantic or for corny people who are extremely intense about life or hypercreative. We all need passion in our lives. We all need moments that make this life worth living, the moments of flow, disconnection, and inner connection with yourself and the divine - regardless of what concept you have about God and the Universe. Passion refers to what you do where time does not exist, where seconds, minutes, and hours are interchangeable. That magic you consider your element, what you don't hesitate to do, you naturally know how to do, and there is no doubt you love to do it. Close your eyes, and try to connect with those passions. Do they easily pop up in your mind? What did you feel passionate about when growing up? What is that thing that you always have been excited to do?

Even if you think you don't have a passion, we all have one or many. You just haven't connected with it yet, or you think it has to be something extraordinary, like playing a musical instrument or painting the ceiling of a church. Please, consider that a passion can be as simple as making cookies, cycling, having deep conversations, or reading. You can think about passions the same way you think about hobbies; this does not necessarily mean all hobbies are passions. You can have hobbies but still not be in love with them, they may not come from your soul, and you practice them because it is a habit or a tradition to share time with your loved ones.

Some life coaches usually recommend people try different things every day or every week during a period to find their elements, like taking new courses, cooking or dancing classes. The famous author and speaker Ken Robison recommends this in his book, *Finding Your Element*. However, even when I think that is great, and you can probably discover your passion by experimenting and trial-and-error, you already know what your passions are. Your purpose and passions have always been inside you and have been calling you your whole life. However, you have not heard them because you have been too busy catching up with the demands of the modern world. Thankfully, now you are taking the time to rediscover them and connect with them.

To start this journey, you will begin by traveling to your childhood; as we saw in the previous chapters, you may find a more authentic version of who you are before you start absorbing the cultural programs that told you what you should become. Then we will explore what moves you most and see if we can start unlocking your purpose. Remember, this may be just one iteration of your passion and purposes, and they will be clearer with time.

Finally, remember that some people may find their purpose and passions in what they do as a job. However, this is only for some. Your purpose and passions may not be related to what you do for a living. Thus, in the next exercises, try not to think about your job, career, diplomas or what you think you are good at. Instead, connect with your dreamer, visionary, and idealist — your authentic self.

Rediscovering Your Inner Child

When you are a teenager, or in your early twenties, people expect you to grow up and to be more mature. However, growing up does not mean being more serious, finding a proper job and start paying your bill. Instead, growing up really means finding yourself again, mentally, physically and emotionally. It never meant stopping enjoying little things, doing goofy things or taking life too seriously. For this reason, you would reconnect with the child you still have inside to find the voices of presence and unconditional happiness you left behind when you had to be "more mature." The thoughts, ideas, experiences and dreams that kid had never left your psyche. Do you remember that kid? —the thoughts, the personality, the games, and the life your consciousness experienced?

Before moving forward with your case, remember how a child behaves or connects with when you saw a three or four-year-old kid for the last time. They are like free birds, completely living in the "now," in the present moment. Kids normally never think about what happened yesterday and their fight with their little sister the week before. Instead, they wake up every morning to embrace the new day discovering, exploring, learning, playing and enjoying every moment. They are not worried about what people think about them when they are in their element, screaming, jumping, or running. Their ego has not yet grown to the point that they are thinking about what they have to do next week or how much homework they must do. Time is still nonexistent like they knew that the only thing that matters is the present moment, which is, in fact, the ultimate truth.

Meditation – The Child in You

Do the breathing exercise we learned in the previous chapter for at least three minutes. After that, close your eyes and try remembering the house, apartment, and neighborhood you lived in when you were 4 to 12. If there was more than one place, pick the one more relevant to you or the one that firsts come to your consciousness. Next, go to where you used to spend most of your time: your room, your parent's room, the family room, or the backyard. Try to travel to the place as if you were there right now. Remember the floor, the landscape, the furniture, the colors, and the textures. Remember the flavors, what you used to eat, the smells of the food cooked by your mother and the person who cared for you. Remember your feelings when playing outside with your friends, cousins and pets, if you have any. Also, remember how you felt when your parents or grandfather scolded you. Remember you! How did you look? How did you behave? And how was your personality?

Move a little further toward the future when you were in middle school. Remember going to school, the bus or the car your parents had to take you to school. Remember the classrooms, the uniform and the clothes you used to wear. Remember your dreams, the questions you were asking, your main concerns, and your biggest fears. Remember your favorite classes and the subjects you enjoyed the most, what you felt proud about, and the main achievements in middle school. Before you continue reading, take a little more time to go to those moments in your life, feel those forgotten things, and how magical it is to time travel. Stay there, as much as you can, to connect deeply.

Now, it is time to create a mind map of your childhood. A mind map is a tool to help you organize ideas around a central thought and in radial symmetry— a central idea that divides into sub-ideas. In the end, you will have a visual diagram of all the ideas, causes, topics, subjects, and in this case, memories.

Take a blank sheet, the bigger, the better, and right in the middle of the sheet, write the macro-memory called "my childhood," then link this macro-memory to four memory types:

- Favorite hobbies and games
- Favorite subjects or classes
- Fears or concerns
- Questions about the world

Then, around each of these memories, write sub-memories for each memory. The mind map is going to look something like this.

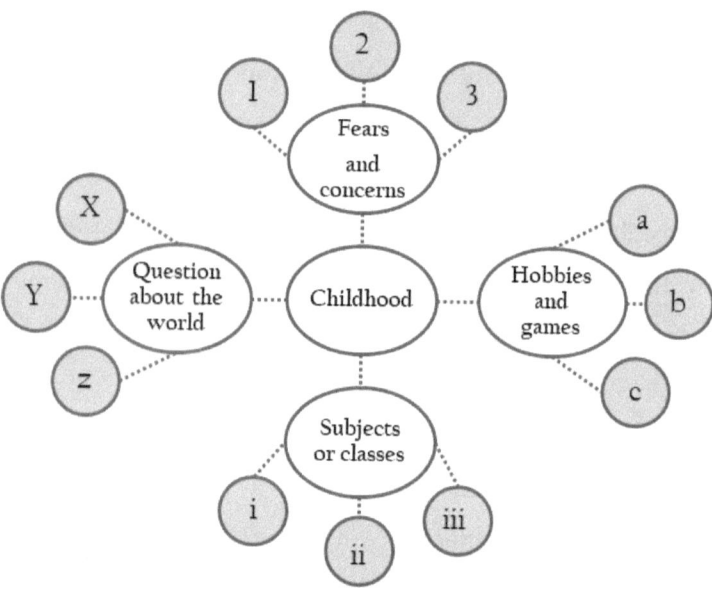

Figure 4 - Childhood Mind Map

I suggest you use these topics for this memory visualization tool, but you can add whatever you feel is most important. In my case, "Questions about the world" were very important to unlock my purpose. Inside the questions that haunted me for many years, the ones that caused more conflicts in my life, and the ones that caused more pain, was the place I found the answers to what I wanted to do and I felt passionate about.

Please don't link whatever you feel are your purpose and passions with what you do in your job or for a living. For now, identify everything that makes your heart beat faster and harder, like hope inside you.

Only Five Minutes

Imagine that you have five minutes to share a message with the world, and you have those minutes to tell humanity why we are here on earth, to reprogram their brains. Whatever you tell them, they will believe it to be true and will implement the changes and improvements you suggest in their life and for the good of humanity. Take a deep breath, close your eyes and think about what that message would be. What do you want others to know that you feel they don't know yet? What is that problem or issue that you want them to solve, that you want them to understand so they can have better lives? What are those things at the bottom of your soul and heart that you want to scream to the rest of the world?

For example, I want to tell people to stop being afraid of finding themselves, of discovering who they are. I want people to stop being afraid of living their lives and becoming whatever they want to become. I want to help people increase their consciousness levels and stop suffering for not being what others want them to be. This book is a representation of what I want to say. This book is a conglomerate of nostalgia after the struggles and all the unconscious pain I had in my life. It is more than two decades of identifying what I wanted to do, or better, what I wanted to be. I know it's not a five-minute message, but just how I express my purpose through my passion —writing.

Try not to think that your passion and purpose must be 100% related to what you do in your job today; they can be two different things. You can still go to the office you don't like, share time with people you don't have anything in common with, and work for a company you don't share your values. The important thing is not to forget who you are. You are not the consultant, not the lawyer, not the accountant. That is just what you do. You are not a wife; you are not the mother; you are not the friend; these are only the relationships you have. You are the awareness in this physical form, right now, in this space-time, with a message to share with the world.

To concretize this five-minute message, rethink why you are here in this universe. Are you here to collect and possess more and more expensive things? Are you here to send your kids to the most expensive school so they can continue with the next stage of collecting more things? Are you here to collect pictures of places and make a checklist of places you have visited? What are you here for? The time we are on earth is just a glimpse of billions of years of evolution, and the earth will be here another billion more. Dedicate this opportunity to be and find yourself, and discover a purpose and a passion that vibrates with your spirit into higher frequencies.

Time, programs, and the history of the world have made you forget who you are, so you have a very important mission with you— to rediscover your real self. If you continue ignoring it and stay with the misconception of the world moving forward, it will be hard to find the happiness or the peace you are seeking within your soul. So, stop here and right now, and give yourself a moment of stillness, presence, and meditation to start rediscovering who you are and why you are here, regardless of what happened tomorrow, the next day, or the next year. Even if you decide to continue where you are right now, if you continue in the same job, house, or neighborhood, always try to remember the five-minute message you want to share with the world every single day of your life. That message may be what you really represent, your biggest value.

You don't have to be Steve Jobs or Nelson Mandela to leave a legacy for the world. You don't need to compare yourself to others because you are unique as your legacy. The message you want to share has the shape and form of your ancestors, past, and experiences. It does not have to be similar or equal to anything. It is only the message you want to share with the rest of the world, the message you want to leave to your children and the people you love. But it has to be clear, as you know your name, your sex, and your nationality. The message you want to share moves your deepest emotions; it can make you cry by only thinking it is possible and that you desperately need to share it. These feelings are the beginning of unlocking your purpose and your passion.

Even when we have a skeptical and pragmatic point of view—the scientist and the rational thinker within you that believes all we are is a mix of chemicals, cells, and organs that send messages to the brain for us to have perceptions and sensations, understand that purpose and passion are not only some New Age made-up concepts. They are within our DNA and are needed for our mental health and connection with others. Trust your instinct. Don't you think it is better to believe that you can send that five-minute message, plus solve the problems that keep you up at night by doing what you enjoy the most? What if all that you dreamed of being as a child and you dream today as an adult can be a reality for you and your loved ones? Does it feel good? Does it feel like something you want to do? Does it feel like something worth fighting?

Do not allow your egoic mind and the fears of your adult life to blind you from the passion for living. You know there is something there, something that is moving in your heart and your soul that you are not able to explain yet. So do not ignore it anymore and start its pursuit.

Exercise – Unlock Your Purpose

At this point of the book, and especially if you have had some insights and done the exercises with your heart, or better yet, with your soul, you have rediscovered many things about yourself. Therefore, you may be ready to unlock your purpose and try the following exercise.

In the middle of a blank paper, like the mind map, write down the question: "What is my purpose?" Then, without thinking and reflecting on what you have learned, start writing answers to that question from your soul. The answer that makes you cry or feel an intense emotional connection is the closest to your purpose. This exercise can last several minutes. But if it has been more than 20 minutes and you still haven't written the phrase, that makes you cry. Stop and try another day again with a different energy level or state of mind.

Chapter 10 – Plan Your Life

Would you tell me, please, which way I ought to go from here?" asked Alice. "That depends a good deal on where you want to get to," said the Cat. "I don't much care where–" said Alice. "Then it doesn't matter which way you go," said the Cat.

- Lewis Carrol, Alice in the wonderland -

With more clarity of your passion and purpose, it's time to start designing your future. Even when it may sound crazy, you should start believing that you are the creator of your life, regardless of the things you cannot control. If you think carefully, where you are today is the result of the decisions you have made and the things you wanted to happen. Nevertheless, in life, there is one fundamental decision between two options: to feel empowered to become the person you are supposed to be or to leave life alone to take with you whatever it wants. And this chapter is to encourage you to choose the first option.

There isn't a coaching program in the world that does not talk about goal setting, and even then, there are many ways to set goals. However, in this program, the goal setting happens after the 7th step of the *Matryoshka Method* in the second section, Reinvent Yourself. You cannot start planning without having luggage ready to embrace the trip. That luggage consists of many things we have already discovered: your values, the meaning of success, the connection with your intuition, your passions, and your purpose statement. Do not worry if you think this luggage is incomplete or feel something is missing; you can always get more things on the way. You will probably discover new values you didn't know were important; you might realize that your passion tasted better with more sugar or that your purpose needed fewer words and more feelings.

Any barrier you put at this point for not acting is an excuse from your ego or fears of your unconscious mind. Sometimes, this excuse relates to your beliefs to stay in that comfort zone full of discomfort. Therefore, it is time to start listening to your soul and expanding your heart to a world of possibilities. In this space is where you will find the main manufacturer of your future rather than in the fears you are starting to discover. Additionally, consider all the costs you are incurring to stay where you are among them, maybe your health, your family and peace of mind. And consider they may be a waste and not an investment if this place differs from where you want to be the next year or in five or ten years.

Before moving forward to start planning your life, I want to uncover three concepts—pleasure, happiness, and joy. You may understand them differently, but these new ideas should be considered moving forward to calibrate your purpose and passion, if necessary.

These three concepts are located in the psyche and according to the consciousness state of each individual—pleasure is in the ego spectrum of things, while real happiness and joy are more on the soul side of things.

Pleasure

Pleasure is those things you desperately want to satiate the lack of something, the feeling of incompleteness, and to feed your ego. Think, for example, about a piece of chocolate cake. If you are not a fan of chocolate like me, think about something that is irresistibly delicious and impossible not to eat for you. The cake is in front of you, and you cannot think about anything other than jumping and eating it. You eat it, satiate your cravings, and still want more of that cake. After a while, you eat not only one piece but the entire cake by yourself. When you see the empty box of that cake, you regret it. You feel bad because you were not supposed to eat that much sugar, you need to start controlling your cholesterol, and you are gaining a lot of weight. The feelings of guilt and shame followed, which are the favorite and lowest energetic feelings of our friend Mr. Ego.

I call this type of pleasure: harmful pleasure. Sometimes, this particular type of pleasure is easily recognizable because it relates to something negative to our bodies or finances, like overeating, alcohol, meaningless sex, and gambling. I say "sometimes" is easy to recognize because many people are still so unconscious of themselves that they cannot even see or accept they are entangled in a negative situation. They know so little about their human nature, past, feelings, minds and souls that they blind themselves even more by justifying their actions. Generally, these justifications have a voice of arrogance and lack of self-love. And in cases like this, the people observing the issue from the outside are the ones who can easily identify a problem, which normally refers to a feeling of emptiness and the need to satiate the lack of something else.

However, another type of pleasure is hard to identify for both the consumer and the observer because it can be confused with the concept of happiness. I call that type of pleasure harmless pleasure. But, as with any pleasure, it also seeks to satiate the lack of something and to feed the ego. These types are not necessarily something you do to your body or inject into your brain, like watching the news all day, and it is more related to the possession of material things.

To understand an example, I will change the chocolate cake example to the most sophisticated car on earth today. Let's imagine that you have the means to afford it. Also, you have worked very hard to buy that car finally. It is your prize for your sacrifice and all the new clients you closed during the year. You deserve it. But let me ask you something, how long will the sensation of happiness last? Hours, days, weeks, months? Did that new car make you feel better at your job or with your spouse? Do you feel less lonely?

Notice that the example of a simple car does not apply if you need to accommodate your family or avoid the three hours commute on an uncomfortable bus. That car is fixing a problem and giving you tranquility and a little peace of mind to continue functioning in this world. I'm talking about the trophy that will make you feel better about yourself, even making you think you are a better person, like if, after that car, you became a worthy human being, and that thing was the only one missing to be happy. Similar situations happen every time you get things you don't need for comfort or survival but to be in fashion and do as others do: the latest smartphone, the bag and the pair of shoes, more Botox, and liposuction.

Don't get me wrong. I'm not saying you cannot get all the things you want or that you cannot celebrate life and success. On the contrary, it would be best to celebrate every little achievement in your life. If you made it, you deserve it. It's more about what you expect to get out of those celebrations.

Happiness is not necessarily circumstantial. And I say not necessarily because if you are in real need or have lost your home or people you loved, it will be more difficult to find happiness. But if you "have it all," sometimes more than you need, and still consider you need more to find joy; it is probably time to stop on the way and realize the real reason for your dissatisfaction is not about having more.

Pleasure, momentary satisfaction, and this fake sensation of happiness are illusions made by your mind with the help of your hormones of accomplishment and pride, dopamine and serotonin. Please make sure to differentiate the ingredients of this cocktail of feelings when you set your goals. Real happiness is a feeling that always comes after a feeling of gratefulness. Plus, happiness is never a goal to be accomplished tomorrow or the next year when you finally get everything you desire. Happiness is something you can only find in the now.

Happiness and Joy

Many believe they will finally be happy when they get that extra thing, finish this goal, get that promotion, gain that salary, and buy that house. This idea is close to the concept of success we spoke of in chapter seven; if something, it is exactly the same. The concept that the invisible hand created, expecting you to stay clinging to the system of what you were told to do, which never was to find real happiness. Real happiness is more related to living your values, achieving your definition of success, and living your passion and your purpose every moment of your life.

Joy is closer to the feeling of peace and is also different from happiness. Joy and peace come with a feeling of surrender and acceptance, which are not similar to resignation and apathy, which are on the left side of our consciousness spectrum. They are unconscious feelings that can only appear when we don't understand all the variables that play into place in the construction of our lives. Those feelings can be experienced when we are the victims of the world and believe there is nothing we can do to change our reality. Those feelings can only flourish when we don't know ourselves and don't embrace our past and history and don't comprehend our place in the universe. In other words, ignorance.

The teaching of Buddhism talks about ignorance and its relationship with pain and suffering. However, this ignorance is separate from knowledge of the external world, knowledge about geopolitics, science, and technology. Buddha was trying to teach us knowledge of ourselves, what we really are, and the mastery of making the unconscious conscious. The task of knowing ourselves is the most important change we can embrace and do to change the world, improve our lives, and achieve the happiness and joy we all cherish. Only when you understand the things that make you suffer, feel bad, or feel down can you accept and surrender to life. Ignorance about the self always ends up in the blame to others, and external circumstances are the sole origin and explanation of our pain and suffering.

I used to do the same, pointing my fingers at people who made me feel bad and blaming others to be the main reason I could not do better. For example, I thought I was not promoted because they did not want to see me in a better position. After all, I was a Latin woman who didn't speak English as they did. However, when I deeply understood my fears and weaknesses, I made myself responsible for my relationship with the universe. When I recognized myself and accepted my flaws and the ones of the world, I started to forgive and release the tension of resentment toward myself and the world around me. To recognize and accept our flaws and weaknesses as part of what we are and love them as part of our inner history is imperative not only to liberate ourselves from the pain that resentment and guilt bring to our lives but also to recognize others as equals and change the requirement of forgiveness into the ability of understanding.

I also understood that I was not excelling as I wanted because I was not giving much in my work due to dealing with stress and anxiety. But it was only when I embraced the path of self-knowledge and started discovering the tones of my soul that I became more aware of the situations that kept me in a negative state of mind. I didn't have anxiety and stress only because of the excess work and pressure from my boss or coworkers. Even when those situations probably numbed my mind and impeded me from hearing what I wanted, the main trigger of my mental instability was the fact that my soul didn't belong to that place and time. Call it science, thousands of years of evolution or hormones, psychology or a soul; whatever the reason, the more conscious I became, the clearer I could see the monster of unhappiness. Accepting unhappiness was hard because it came with a feeling of failure. And even when today, I have a different idea about failure; at that time, it felt like I was holding the weight of the entire universe on my shoulders. It was not easy to see the eyes of this monster of unhappiness and dissatisfaction in front of me. However, I could only start defeating it by acknowledging it existed and how it looked.

The little door for change, joy, and peace comes from understanding why you are thinking what you are thinking and feeling what you are feeling. However, you need to understand also that events will go as you expected, and people will act in the opposite way. Learning to surrender and accept the universe is crucial when things go unexpectedly and wrong. The universe has a perfect cosmic organization—Dharma, as some ancient eastern cultures call it. We belong to something bigger than we imagine, and things are not just happening against us. Ultimately, the only option when we believe the world is falling apart is to empower ourselves, trust our purpose and align the universe toward the world we want: cause and effect.

I want you to think about your ideal life. A life where you know you will find happiness, joy, and peace. Remember to be critical and don't include the stuff you desire only. Include your thoughts and your feeling as well. Connect with the emotions around the life you will have, the goals you will accomplish, the message you want to send to the world, your values, and how you changed your relationship with life—your new mindset.

Meditation – Programming Your Perfect Day

Imagine your perfect day. Imagine how and where you wake up. Imagine your room and who is with you at home. Don't think about when in the future; our brain does not understand what was in the past and what is in the near future or ten years. To prove you so, we can feel happy and feel joy while remembering things, or we can get very sad and worried imagining things that have not even happened, so it does not matter when in time, this can be your perfect morning in four weeks or a year.

Wake up, walk towards a window, look out the window, and admire what you see. Feel grateful, feel at peace, and complete. Think about the first thing you do after experiencing this—you have a lot of energy, and your spirit cannot wait to live this day. Where do you go after that? Who are you meeting with during the morning? Who are you having breakfast with, and what are you having for breakfast? Taste the flavors, feel the breeze and the sun if you are outside, or feel the warmth and the texture of your clothes if you are inside. How do you spend your day? Do you leave your home, why, and how? How was your work day or your business, or you didn't work at all? Where do you expend all the energy during the afternoon? Feel your emotions and be aware of which hormones are leading your day.

What are the sensations you feel when arriving back home at the end of the evening to have dinner? Who are you having dinner with, and what is the main topic of the conversation? What do you do before going to bed? Do you read your favorite book by yourself or share it with someone? What is the feeling when you feel the sheets touching your skin? What do you feel about waking up tomorrow and setting your alarm? What are you expecting to dream that night?

Doesn't it feel great to imagine and think about a perfect day? What would you do to live that day almost every day of your life?

Finally, I want you to connect with an idea. Whatever is in your mind has the power to become a reality; that's how every dream comes true; it starts with a thought. You are about to write down the plan to make that day a reality. And if the result of this plan could be guaranteed to you, you will do whatever it takes and work on every step. However, the only single person that can guarantee that is yourself.

Reconsidering Money

We have already spoken about money and our relationship with it, which is one of the biggest struggles for many people. Most people spend their lives thinking, planning, and living around money. Not only because people may have real financial issues but because egos are obsessed with it even when they don't need more to live. Sometimes it feels like making money was our sole goal when we came into this world. In other words, if you had all the money in the world or enough to have a better life than what you have today, you would not go to a job you hate daily.

With this in mind, try not to plan your future with the limitation of this resource because you are framing your whole life with a constraint. When your limit your life to one resource, you are not designing a life you want; you are designing the life you think you are obliged to have. Yes, money is vital in this materialistic world but try to put your dreams first for a moment. Additionally, when the purpose is clear, you understand that life is beyond money and magical things will happen. We also know now that money to buy things won't make us happy; joy comes from other factors, like a balanced life and living our values. So, when planning, dreaming and visualizing your future, do not put money as the mainframe, as the limitation.

Reconsidering Your Capabilities

Since we were young, we have all been told that we are not good at certain things, that we have limited capabilities and limited knowledge, so we have to keep studying and keep spending money on school and certifications so one day we can be good at something. However, you already know that often the things said to you may be programs that someone told you according to their limiting beliefs or a cultural checklist of requirements. Programs that you decided to believe in because you didn't know better, but that are not necessarily true.

If you think the only way to get the job you want or to be promoted is by expending a lot of time, energy, and money on a new diploma, let's stop for a second and reconsider this belief. First, many people are not hired or get the job they have a diploma for or have been prepared for years, especially in business. In my case, for example, I'm an engineer who ended up doing accountants' work. Universities and education entities give you the basics, so you have a broad knowledge of a topic. This idea does not pretend to undermine the institutions and people that have decided to invest the value of their household into schooling; I only want you to consider that a diploma will not necessarily take you there where you want to go.

Additionally, have you ever met someone with a job you know you can do better and have better qualifications to excel? The world is full of these situations. The only difference between you and the person with that job is not only the qualifications and the aptitudes but the fact that this person is certain that they are good at what they do and has learned how to spread that security around them.

If there is a skill or some specific knowledge you want to improve to get the job you want, I'm pretty sure that if there is something you are passionate about, really passionate about, you can do it yourself. For example, let's imagine that you want to change your career from law to marketing, and you are afraid of moving since you don't have that piece of paper that says you know about marketing. Nevertheless, today we can find online information, books, and seminars similar to what people at Georgetown University in Washington D.C. read—probably not for free or cheap. But still, if you want to know and become an expert on a certain topic, you can do it; you only need the determination to change the belief that you cannot do it. Of course, I'm not saying if you want to become an engineer designing a rocket for people to go to Mars or to become a neurosurgeon, you don't need specific training from an expert. I'm talking just about marketing and business.

Imagine you finally got the interview with the company's marketing director you always wanted to work for because your resume shows you know about marketing. And instead of telling the Director of Marketing that you have a diploma from Georgetown University, you say from the bottom of your heart:

"I'm passionate about marketing and made myself an expert on the topic. I took courses online offered by the best institutions in the field. I also researched the most important study cases used by the top universities worldwide, including China, Europe, and Latin America. I not only read them but reviewed and analyzed each one of them. I have already studied most books on disruptive marketing available on Kindle, around 20. And I wrote a paper about the topic, published in one of the top five business magazines, which were impressed by how I developed the difference between marketing in

first-world countries with third-world countries. Here! There is a copy of the paper."

If, after this speech, they don't hire you, let me tell you something, that's not the company you are supposed to be, and you should find a new one, more aligned with the power you have within yourself.

Do not limit your plans to what you have done during the last few years and the capabilities you think you have. You can do it gracefully if you feel it and are linked with your purpose and passion. Trust me, you only need to believe in yourself and believe you can do it. You cannot know that you are amazing in marketing if you have never tried it. And if someone told you that you are not, prove to them how wrong they were. Probably what you want to do next is not open-heart surgery. This is business, and business is also about intuition and creativity. So, stop playing the game of the checklist and open your mind to the future of the business world. If you are passionate about something, go for it, don't let life pass before your eyes without even trying.

Cut the Chains of Your Past and Change Your Relationship with the Future

After understanding what happiness really means and that we must not limit ourselves before planning the life where we know joy will be found, I want you to remember one last thing. What has happened before in your life, what happened to your parents, what your ancestors shared with your grandfather, has nothing to do with you anymore if you decide it won't. You now know you can free yourself from that; you don't need to keep the same beliefs and mindset. You have all you need to reach the freedom, peace, and life you want. You have the canvas and the oils to paint your future and whatever you want from it. You have the tools you need to do so, and the most important is you — your authentic self.

You have been the creator of your life all this time, and you will be the creator of your future from today until the last day of your life. Use all the colors you want on the canvas; stop being black-and-white, and add red, yellow, and pink to your life. The power of consciousness is the best gift you will ever give yourself and to your loved ones, and it is the superpower you will use now to write down the goals of each aspect of your life. You will read those goals in five years and exclaim: "OMG, I did do all I wanted, and the universe gave much more than I expected."

Nothing you do with the power of your soul, heart, and consciousness will go wrong, even when your ego tells you otherwise. You are the painter of your own life. Let's create a sketch of that masterpiece right now. This life you are living is the only life you are certain about; let's make the best of it.

Personal Story – Crying on the floor

One day in 2017, one of the most amazing revelations of my life was about to happen. I was at the point of figuring out, again, what to do with my life. So I opened the old journal I had started years ago to resume brainstorming goals and ideas to transform my life. I accidentally opened a page where I had written my goals seven years ago—the page's title was goals for the next five to 10 years. When I started reading them, I was astonished to find out that every little thing I had written on that piece of paper had become real, or I was on the path to making that happen. When I continued reading about every goal and dream that came true, I felt so weak in my legs that I had to sit on the floor and cry. I had not opened that journal for years and had not read those goals hanging on my bedroom door. I even had forgotten I ever wrote them. Those goals were self-programmed into my subconscious or tattooed on my soul, so I could keep navigating life with them deep inside me.

Never stop dreaming. It is always a good time to refresh your goals and dreams. Also, remember to be precise about where, how, and why you will be in the next year to ten years. Precision is vital because the subconscious speaks with symbolism and metaphors mind can create as many interpretations as possible about thoughts and desires.

Exercise – Planning Your Life

For each one of the aspects of your life, define a goal and visualize yourself living that. Make sure the visualization is deep, just as in the exercise we did when we pictured the best day of your life. Then, set specific goals, numbers, names, and deadlines for each goal, all using a positive context.

For example, if you want to lose weight, think and write down your ideal weight and your ideal percentage of body fat. Do not think about the amount you want to lose, or do not write it like "stop eating sugar and fries." Instead, connect to how great you will look and feel, why you want to do it and how you will enjoy it. Focus on positive actions, like eating delicious fruits and healthy broccoli, enjoying exercising every day and learning to cook delicious and healthy meals.

If you want to live in the countryside, in a calm and quiet area with less traffic and congestion, be as specific as you can—the sector, next to which river and how many rooms your will house has. Also, if there are things you can do right away, do them. Then, contact the realtor and start looking for the dream quiet house, regardless of how much money they approved at the bank or if you have how to pay for it. Remember, money is not your limit.

If you want to retire when you are 50, imagine the exact number you need in your bank account, with cents and everything, so you can live until you are 100 years old with all the comfort you deserve. Abstain from thinking about how much work you must do or how impossible it will be.

If you want to help orphans, define how many you want to help and the time frame, and define how and what you want them to become after you help them. Don't think about how hard it would be.

If you want to start your jazz band, define when you would start practicing and contact the potential members. Define how many songs you want to compose and how many gigs per month you will have. Refrain from thinking about your lack of practice and how hard it is to find good musicians.

Finally, for each aspect and each goal, close your eyes and visualize yourself and the ones you love accomplishing the goal, but this time connect with the feelings. Connect to your heart and the sensations of your body having that life. Speak to every part of yourself, your fears, your ego, and your soul, and request that they feel confident about this future and the path you are designing.

If there are things on that list you can start doing today, of which I am certain, pick up the phone now and make that call — Test drive the car you want, call your mother now and start rebuilding that relationship, call the friend who told you about opening that business, and visit the website of the university you want to apply to, whatever you feel. Please do it now; there is no future; we only have this very second, this exact moment.

Remember, do not limit yourself. The mind is infinite and abundant. Play with the superpower of imagination and creativity. There is no charge for dreaming; if the plans and results feel scary, even better. Dream big. Only consider massive transformations instead of littler changes. For example, finding a job that pays 20% more or remodeling the bathroom is short for the power you have within yourself. And remember not to be afraid of the possibility of this not being a reality, don't even consider that. Better to be foolish for dreaming big than a pessimistic and self-doubting person who only listens to fear. Silence your ego as much as possible so you ignore its limiting beliefs, at least during this exercise.

Chapter 11 – The Best Version of You

"Your eyes are not really windows through which you look out into the world. Your eyes are cameras that send electronic images of the world into you."

- Michael A. Singer, The Untethered Soul -

At this point in the book, you have already identified, philosophized, or at least dreamed about what your life will be like and are considering making significant changes in your life. You know a little more about yourself, your fears, and your mindset, and the cool thing is that you know all about your future—you just designed it. Best of all, it is time to start putting this plan, these ideas, and your dreams into action. To start this journey, you also know life will unfold differently, problems will always arise, and people will react in mysterious ways as soon as you start making changes in your life. The Universe will test you, challenging you to choose this new direction in life. So, there are additional things I want to share with you to help you become the best version of yourself and strengthen your superpowers.

You don't need to change who you are; you are not looking to become another person; you are only trying to discover your real self and send the judge and the pessimist inside you to sleep. The idea is to change the perception of the things unfolding in front of you every moment. Your relationship with life and the Universe, and the things that happen to you every moment or the people you are interacting with, sets the pace for everything else. Becoming the best version of yourself is the third step of the *Matryoshka Method*, in the section, Reinvent Yourself, and the 9th overall.

Your Relationship with Life and the Universe

We have talked a little bit about Dharma. We spoke of it in chapter six during the example of the person going to work late who runs out of gas and again in chapter 10 when we explored the concepts of joy and peace. We also touched on Dharma when we tried to picture all the things that happened for us to be where we are now—our ancestors, our decisions, and the decisions of others. Even though it has many meanings and interpretations in eastern religions, we will define Dharma as the perfect order of the Universe and all the things within it. It's like this invisible hand that allows life to unfold. It is not a supernatural force that controls life, but more like an infinite number of events happening on all the levels of our existence, from the atoms and hormones to the decisions we make, from our planet spinning for a day to happen to the galaxies traveling through space.

We have used the example of the evolution of our species to understand that our history as a modern civilization and the things we are exposed to today are different than the environment our ancestors were exposed to during our lives. But what if we move that understanding not only to the history of humans but to the history of the entire Universe? For this, I will use the metaphor of the cosmic calendar from one of my favorite inspirations growing up, Carl Sagan.

Imagine that the history of the Universe is comprised of a calendar year. The explosive start of the Universe was the first second of January 1st of that calendar year, 13.8 billion years ago (13,800,000,000 years). Then billions of years of gas and matter traveled and formed space-time until they started gathering together as galaxies. Our galaxy, the Milky Way, was not formed until May of that cosmic calendar, and our solar system was not until September. Life started on earth not long after the earth was formed, in October. The dinosaurs disappeared the day before New Year's Eve, on December 30th. The early human ancestor, Lucy, appeared slightly before 10 p.m. on December 31st. Gautama Buddha died five seconds before midnight. And modern history started somewhere in the last second of the cosmic calendar. All the scientific documented discoveries, all the technology and robotics, all the intercontinental travels and colonization, the world wars and Marxism, genetics studies and quantum physics, all the movies and symphonies happened at 11:59:59 on December 31st of the cosmic calendar.

This eternal and mystic change is Dharma. The perfection of the Universe and the transformation of everything unfolding in front of our eyes. Every atom, every cell, every animal, every leaf, every neuron, every human, every second of life. Your life, however, is a glimpse compared to the time the Universe has been here. When we consider all the possibilities of what could have happened, life is a spectacular gift, even when we can observe a fraction of it. There are millions and millions of things that happened for us to be where we are right now, and many others are happening right now regardless of our awareness or not. The Universe and life on earth are miracles, just being witnesses of that miracle should be enough for us to be grateful for every little thing that happens to us. Just think of something as simple as the tree in the corner of your house or your favorite park. Think about all the things that had to happen for that tree to be there and for you to be observing that tree. If you think about the odds of that happening, it is just as unlikely as your existence. It's a miracle, the most wonderful one.

However, we don't appreciate that anymore and may have never adequately appreciated it. We took for granted the wonders of being humans, having this complex brain, and having the superpower of controlling what we believe, think, dream, and how we embrace life. We have the remarkable gift of being conscious to appreciate what the Universe has to offer, maybe a level of consciousness that the bird resting on a tree does not have. And being aware of this power should be enough to be grateful. But unfortunately, our minds and ego seem to be in a constant fight to keep us stuck in old patterns of thought that we have not taken responsibility for, to cut the cycle of perpetual ignorance.

The house you don't like, the fight you had with someone you loved last night, your traumatic childhood, the boss that makes your life impossible, your uncle dying last year, your divorce, your troublemaker son, your greasy hair, your weight, your lack of performance at the office, your laziness, the car accident last month, your insecurities, your fears, the ugly bus you need to take to work, the kids who bullied you at school, the teacher you hated, your conflicting mother, the friend you cannot stand anymore, your grandfather's cancer, your big mouth, your lack of dancing skills, that missed opportunity, your lack of character, the few zeros in your bank account, the dog you loved getting sick, your loneliness, the job you hate, the career you regret, the money you lost in the stock market, the boyfriend who left you, the decision you shouldn't have made, the insults you said, the friend that never called back—love it all, you have no other option than to love it. If you keep complaining, regretting, hating, unforgiving, and not accepting your life, you will continue to suffer now and for the rest of your life. Those things did not happen to you as a punishment. All those things happen for you to witness them, to live them.

This glimpse you have is all the variables of the Universe gathering together for you to experience it. It's what you are living in this physical world and reality at this very moment. Love it with all the bad sensations and discomfort it brings. Love it with all of the flaws, all of the tears, and all of the unfairness. All of that happened to you because you were here to be part of it, to create this great little story, to build the person you are and the person you will become, to learn the lessons, to get stronger, to learn how to love. Love it. It is you. It is your Universe.

When I share this idea with the people I work with, my friends and my family, I've received reactions like: "This is impossible, there are always problems, you cannot ignore that you have a problem," "How you are going to accept someone dying and act as nothing happened?" "There are humans killing each other in Syria and people robbing and raping innocents; how can you love that or be happy with that?" And these same challenges are the juncture where you understand that you have to love it all, when the magic happens and when you understand who will play the leading role in your life: the blinded and unconscious you, full of fears and judgment, or the conscious you, who understands the perfection of the Universe, from which we only get to see some of the nanoseconds of our cosmic calendar.

It is your choice; it is your decision. And by the way, it is one of the most important decisions you will ever make in your life. Do you want to be the complainer who criticizes how other people drive and yells at the traffic jams, or do you want to be the driver who enjoys the music or landscapes and is still amazed by the invention of the automobile? Do you want to be the person who complains because it is raining or the one who is grateful because our plants need rain to grow? Do you want to be the person who posts on social media against the current president every day, or do you want to be the person who works for a purpose every day so that we can build a better world? Do you want to be the person who feels like a victim of the Universe or the person who understands that you are a miracle and is thankful for every breath of every second? Do you want to be the person who complains every time the alarm sounds on Mondays or the person who is grateful to have a new day to enjoy? Do you want to keep resentment against the person who disappointed you, or are you going to be the person who understands that we are all driven by our unconscious minds and have different universes, therefore fears, frustration, and doubts? The decision of the version you want to become is on you—love vs. fear.

However, life always gets in the way. Life will get in the way and will get hectic. Regardless of your meditation practice and the change in your thoughts, you will still experience discomfort, pain, fear, resentment, and anger. Even when many things commence to heal because you are now more aware of your past and have discovered many things about your unconsciousness, you still feel unhappy, incomplete, and frustrated. And the answer is not to continue meditating for ages once you find peace. The secret and direct path to joy and peace is to fall in love with the path of spiritual growth to the connection with the now: your surroundings, body, and feelings.

Your Relationship with Your Feelings

You are made of emotions and feelings. Every problem we think we have results from a bad feeling, a discomfort. You know you have a problem, are angry or feel sad when there is discomfort in your body, something telling you that there is something wrong, and it's opposite to feelings of joy, happiness, peace, or other positive emotions. Emotions are so strong that you forget that they are just that—feelings—and get lost in the discomfort.

But you are not those emotions and feelings; you are just the witnesses of those emotions. Negatives or positive, those emotions feed you information about something happening within your system. For example, think about the feeling of hunger. It is just how your body tells you to charge yourself with energy. However, that sensation is not telling you you will die of starvation. We know that even if you don't eat for a day or three days, you won't die. However, we interpret the sensation of hunger as something extremely negative, even when it may be true that the sensation of hunger feels like a hurry to eat. People often react impulsively to that sensation, almost like it is the end of the world. People have convinced themselves that hunger changes their mood and makes them angry, or they cannot concentrate if they don't eat. They are giving it more power than it has nowadays. In our civilization, and thankfully for many of us, it is just a matter of changing the thought. If you already know that nothing happens if you don't eat for a while, except if you have a special condition, you don't need to cause additional distress to yourself. Spending that energy on something that provides peace may be more compassionate for you and the people around you.

It is important to listen to our animal instincts and respect them. They have thousands of hundreds of years of evolution and wisdom. We need to understand them and be conscious of their meaning and how they affect our psychology and behavior, but not necessary to be controlled by them. We are not only animals; we are conscious beings capable of interpreting the Universe like any others species. Sometimes it is as simple as interpreting the Universe more beautifully.

Do the exercise, and the next time you are hungry in a restaurant, and the food is taking longer than expected, stop for a second instead of pushing the waiter or complaining and put things in perspective. You will see how your emotions will change instantaneously. This exercise will be an easy experience of how you are in control of yourself.

This automatic reaction to hunger is similar to the responses when facing other negative emotions or unknown sensations. We are so immersed in these sensations we feel that we must get out of it immediately, without stopping for a minute to embrace the emotion. Other times, instead of escaping, we choose disorientation, preoccupation, and impatient. This reaction, however, is normal. As most of us were never told how to deal with emotions, the intensity of the feelings feels like the end of the world. Therefore, the lack of awareness of the self triggers an instinctive reaction, whether to feed our pain with more worries and suffering that reinforce the state of victimhood or to escape that state of mind immediately. We rarely choose to observe the sensations, feeling compassion for ourselves and doing something to feel better and remain calmer.

You know that you are not going to die for having a feeling. Negative emotions can only affect your health after years of accumulated pain, suffering or negative energy storage. However, negative feelings and emotions are not our enemies; they are messengers warning us about our state of mind, especially our unconscious which includes: fears, frustrations, past, and attachments. It is one of the most powerful tools for self-work and self-knowledge, to fight the ignorance that makes us suffer, and to liberate our souls. You only need to learn how to benefit from that tool given to you the day you were born; it is your intrinsic design.

One of the teachings from Buddhism and other spiritual paths is not to name feelings. We are not even sure that whatever you feel as anxiety, despair, or depression is the same as the rest of the world feels. The only thing we all know is that it doesn't feel right or uncomfortable. When you name your feelings, you are given more power to them, and your brain will have more reasons to feel miserable. As we have created a preconception about the word's meaning, you are reinforcing your brain to go into a reactive mode, which is usually unnecessary.

When negative emotions are triggered, and you start feeling the energy released into your body, don't do anything but observe the sensations. Observe the emotion, and don't react. Instead, move your awareness towards what is happening to your body, and observe the sensations experienced. Sometimes it is not obvious to see how adrenaline and cortisol react in the body, but the more you learn to stop, observe and be patient, the more the negative feelings will pass through your system instead of staying and ruining your day.

When people are triggered, the skin may change colors, the heartbeat could increase, and the hands can get cold and sweaty. Other times, people may feel weak because their blood pressure decreases or their breathing increases. Typically, nanoseconds after a trigger, people instantly react: answering back, screaming or slamming the doors. On top of that, some physical reactions are followed by a reaction within the mind. For example, anger and frustration invade the thought space to create additional ideas to fuel the sensation or justify the physical reaction. Others close themselves up immediately, don't talk, and resist the sensation by unconsciously escaping, whether with entertainment, cigarettes, alcohol, or tons of sugar. But when we give ourselves seconds of stillness and awareness of the body, our organs, and our physical sensations and listen to our thoughts. Reactions are less likely, and you will certainly act more healthily. This practice is not to deny the emotion or suppress the energy. You are just opening the room to awareness and controlling the automatic reactions you will probably regret or feel shame about.

When you focus on your physical body and understand that what is happening inside you is just a release of hormones or energy that make you feel discomfort, the result will never be to feel more negativity. The awareness of your body and the understanding of your chemical reactions help your mind to recognize the origin of the sensations to release negative energy before it is spread in your system. After you observe the sensation, without judging the situation that originates it, you have only one option: learning from it. Our brain stores everything we experienced growing up, and most of those experiences rely upon our unconscious, our subconscious and the instinct that evolved millions of years. Those experiences are stored with sensations, and the energy stored is released every time a trigger occurs. Most negative sensations are not because of what just happened: the e-mail, the discussion, the insult, or the misunderstanding. Instead, these sensations are reactions to the fear and frustration stored deep within ourselves.

For example, please think about an offense or something a person told you that you thought was disrespectful and made you uncomfortable. For example, a criticism from your partner because she or he didn't like how you dressed up one day. Maybe your top was too short, or your makeup was too strong. When you think about that moment, it could make you feel extremely irritated and upset. You could have aggressively reacted because you felt unworthy or even though your partner no longer loves or respects you. However, getting upset is not the only possible reaction to that situation. There may be people who genuinely don't care what others think; not even their partners or Queen Elizabeth II would disturb them.

Different reactions happen because we all have different life experiences stored in our minds and bodies, creating distinct impressions of the same situation. For example, our fears differ greatly from our next-door neighbors, partners, and even siblings. In the Yogi tradition, these impressions are understood as stored energy, called Samskaras. So every time your body reacts or overreacts to a situation or an experience, it is because the Samskara has been triggered—in the previous example, in a negative way.

Returning to the example of the reaction when your partner criticized you, in which you got upset or overreacted. What happens in the system is the unleashing of energy of a memory of the past. For example, when you were a kid, your father probably told you something about how you looked, and that was the first time you felt unworthy or ugly. That energy, and the reason you felt so bad, got stored in your system. The information remains stored in your subconscious mind and your body, even when you don't remember that your father ever criticized you.

For this reason, when you have a similar experience, the same energy is triggered, and you will get irritated and react almost automatically. This reaction happens not only when someone offends you but for every experience —the first time you tried ice cream, had a kiss, won an award in middle school or the first time others kids bullied you. These Samskaras are an expression of your unconscious mind ruling your life and emotions. This explains why sometimes you get upset without even knowing or feeling you wake up on the wrong side of the bed. What triggers or generates a negative sensation or feeling, like what others think about you, is generally never the real reason for your unconscious reactions. They are called unconscious reactions because you don't know the real reason for your anger or frustration. And even when your mind tries to come up with an explanation, the root of the sensation could have been stored ages ago.

In neurology, this unconscious reaction can be the response of the neurons' synapses or connections. They are formed after a determined experience. These connections and characteristics are known as Hebb's rule. This rule also states why changing established connections between neurons is difficult. Once a synapse has been strengthened through the long-term repetition of responses, the synapse becomes more integrated into the brain's neural circuitry. However, these brain pathways and unconscious reactions can be reconfigured, for example, by observing the feeling and becoming aware of the energy released instead of automatically reacting to the body's sensations. This exercise will teach your mind that it does not need to get upset, angry or violently react when triggered. Your brain will know it does not need to run again through the same synapses and can form new ones that imply observing and letting the energy go. The more you tune in with your body, the more assertive you become to catch sensations and reactions before being expressed or spread in the entire body.

Observing your emotions while meditating or during daily activities not only helps to reconfigure the connections in the brain but also helps you in the conversion of the unconscious into the conscious. During the nanoseconds of observation, you can also start listening to what your mind says. Whether it is your ego or intuition, information is being released to be grasped by our conscious mind. This information can contain the justifications of the ego, but also information from where the energy was stored for the first time or the collection of situations of your childhood that accumulated energy for a long time. Awareness of this information will clarify the mind's panorama, speed up the healing and raise your self-consciousness.

Take every trigger as an opportunity to know yourself and ask your intuition why you are mad about that little thing that ruined your day, week, decade, or your entire life. These are opportunities to discover the hidden pain and bring it to the light — to your consciousness. Identifying the situations that trigger you, understanding your subconscious reactions, the pain you have accumulated in your lifetime, and the root of suffering are the starting point for healing and building the path to your inner peace.

When you continue reacting to every situation, your mind and body will not understand there is no need to react, and your pathways will straighten and straighten. Consequently, changing dramatic and unnecessary reactions to meaningless things will be more difficult. And with more time, your anger and pain will transform into deeper suffering and resentment. In decades, you will wonder why you ended up old, embittered, with no friends or family, and blaming the Universe for your destiny. Therefore, changing the relationship with your emotions is one of the most meaningful expressions of self-love in the realm of spiritual growth.

The Universe will continue doing what it has to be, our human nature will keep doing what it was designed to do, and life will continue unfolding every second for the rest of your life. So the time to start changing your relationship with all of it is here and now. Don't wait until tomorrow to reconnect with the beauty in life. Don't wait until tomorrow to understand your feelings. Don't wait until you are promoted and get more money to stop complaining and reacting to everything around you. Don't wait until it is too late to love and love yourself; you will be missing the "whole point."

Your Relationship with Others

We discussed in chapter six that your relationship with others reflects your relationship with yourself. When you are at peace with yourself and your feelings, having a bad relationship with others is hard. However, this statement does not mean negative people don't exist. There are still many people out there that are not looking for healing or answers about themselves. They have left their egos to rule their lives without acknowledging it and may understand a previous version of the Universe. And this is fine; every person has a different journey, and we are not here to judge that path. However, you are here to protect yourself and to understand that it is in the hands of the more conscious ones the responsibility of managing certain situations. As the famous phrase in the movie Spiderman says: "with great power comes great responsibility."

Try an exercise with me. Take your mind to a moment in your current or previous job when you felt disrespected by your supervisor. For example, he or she gave you negative feedback in front of others, and you felt humiliated, and they did not get your back when you needed it. Connect with that moment the best you can and try to choose again where you want to stand. Do you want to be upset with that person, feel angry, and keep judging them? Or do you want to let it go and not get attached to the negative feelings and sensations of that memory?

The only person being affected by those feelings is you, not your supervisor or your coworkers. If some people can do something to humiliate or mistreat you, it is because there is an obvious lack of awareness. They may also lack empathy and may not be conscious of your well-being. Even though you will never understand why people act in a certain way, it is your responsibility to understand that as the owner of your feelings, it is your sole responsibility to make yourself feel better.

Additionally, when you are that people act from their fears and their ego, there is not a lot of room for judgment and anger. Understanding that they may be on a different path of transformation, personal growth, and emotional intelligence will also give you peace. However, this understanding does not mean to do anything or put your head down when attacked. On the contrary, you must stand up for yourself and advocate to be respected, and set boundaries. This understanding means that anybody's unconscious reactions should not strongly affect you. You can discharge the negative energy from others out of your system by observing, understanding and letting go.

However, a good relationship with others is not about forgiveness either, at least from now on. There is nothing you have to forgive. Instead, it is about understanding that most people don't want to harm you directly and are acting out of their subconscious. Remember, people's subconscious is the biggest puppeteer of their behavior, reactions and emotions.

When reaching this point of the book, you have enhanced the superpower of consciousness. Benefit from it to be the best version of yourself and have a lighter life, with more love for yourself and compassion for others. Practice love and compassion everywhere, not only in your workplace. Try it with your family, in the street with strangers, and with your significant other. It is not worth it to continue attaching our lives to little situations, bad feelings, or the "unfairness" of the Universe. Remember, there is no such thing as unfairness; this is just another idea our surroundings planted in our minds.

Your relationship with the Present moment

The only bit of truth, probably the single one I can ensure in this book, is that the only thing you have is *the present moment*. The present moment is the only thing you will ever own; it is your most valuable possession. The possession and your relationship with it will detonate everything in your life because it is the door to the future you are expecting to have. Additionally, the present moment is the only place where you experience happiness and joy; thus, your relationship with it defines a life worth living.

Being in the present moment is when your mind is not in the past or the future. It's being fully conscious of what is happening here and now. So if you look around you now, you will probably be in a room, on a train, in a cafe, in your bed having a cup of tea or a glass of wine, and chilling while reading a book. No big problems are coming after you right on this second. Even the biggest problem you think you have— an argument with someone you love, financial problems, or health situations — doesn't exist outside your mind. At this present moment and space and time, the argument with that person is already in the past; they are not entering your house to tell you that you are losing your house for not paying your mortgage and whatever issue you have with your health, you might not be in the operating room so that they can save your life. (If you happen to be reading this book while you are having surgery, I'm glad that this is the book you decide to keep with you while very sick, it may help you.)

Everything you remember now and whatever you think will happen is only a thought and an idea in your mind, nothing else. It is real and exists because you can witness it, but it is not true in this space-time. At this moment, nothing is happening directly to you. You happen to be in the company of this book and your drink.

Moving forward, whenever you think you have a problem, immediately remind yourself that it is only in your head. If the problem is in the past, connect with the memory and choose again how you want to feel about that moment and tell yourself a story of power, not victimhood. If the problem is in the future and it has yet to happen, remember that 99% of the things that keep us awake at night will never happen. And, connect to your future self and ask for advice on avoiding the risks or problems you think may happen. Through this, you can create a more positive visualization of future outcomes.

So far, I'm sure you know the techniques to be in the present moment. Let me remind you: observing your thoughts without judgment, meditation, yoga, and observing your feelings and your reaction to them—all of these techniques help you be in the now, get out of your egoic mind, and raise your level of consciousness. If you remember our consciousness diagram, being in the now is on the same side as love and awareness. You can also be in the present moment by returning to your body. This technique is one of the steps we learned in the meditation tool of chapter number eight. First, however, I want to share why it is an important tool and other forms of connecting with the body to help you during extreme stress, anxiety, and physical or emotional pain.

Feeling your body is one of the most straightforward ways to come into the now. Because when you are in your body, you are only in the present moment. You cannot be in the future, you cannot be in the past, and you cannot be in your egoic mind. So try it briefly—close your eyes and feel your internal body. Feel what is happening under your skin. You have trillions of cells moving in your organs and muscles and working for you to breathe, circulate your blood, and digest food. It is normal not to feel much of your inner, but this situation is strange at the same time. How is it possible that we cannot feel what is inside us and has been with us for as long as we can remember? And the reason is simple and is not because we are not meant to feel our inner body; it is because nobody ever taught us how to connect with the body, at least not in our modern western culture. Feeling your inner body takes practice, but the more you meditate, the more you become aware of it.

You can also work by paying more attention to your other senses. Paying more attention to the flavors of the food you are eating. Paying more attention to the smells in your room and the places you enter and paying more attention to the sound of your surroundings. To create this awareness, you need to move your attention to the sensations and the senses themselves. For example, instead of simply drinking a cup of coffee, connect to every sip, the smell, the teats, the temperatures of the coffee and the cup, and the liquid touching your tongue and passing through your throat. Every sip brings information to your brain, grasp that information and observe. Feel like you are having that cup of coffee for the first time. Add all the curiosity you need to understand how it feels before, during and after you drink it. It feels like your life is in slow motion.

Frequently practicing these techniques creates new pathways in the brain and counteracts certain unconscious behaviors, such as being in a hurry all the time. This technique is so powerful that some people stop eating certain foods or smoking after only days of practice. Most of them were not aware enough to realize that they disliked the food's flavor or the sensation of smoking. For example, I started enjoying the sounds of the birds outside my window for the first time.; today, I recognize more than four different species of birds and the time of the day they sing. The fridge in my house is a new friend I never thought I would have; it became a powerful tool to control my awareness during my daily meditation. Finally, I discovered I didn't love strong coffee; my automatic mode never realized it was too bitter, so today, I drink it soft.

You can also start cultivating a new relationship with your skin, the sense of touch. There is indescribable magic in the organ that covers your entire body. For example, feeling the friction of the cotton of the shirt you are wearing now, observing the water running on your hands when you are washing them, sensing the hot water running down every part of your skin when you are showering, perceiving the friction with the bed sheets when you are lying down, detecting the warm sunlight on your face, and noticing the wind caressing your skin.

As you can see, you can connect to your body while meditating and in your daily activities. Little by little, there more you practice, it will become a habit for you to stop being in that automatic mode and become more aware of what is happening in your "now." I highly recommend these body awareness techniques when you are under stress, pain, and anxiety. It does not take much effort, it's easy, and it's free. Try it, and you will discover the magic contained in your life's most valuable instrument, your body.

Becoming the best version of yourself is the opposite of constant disappointment due to the things happening around you. Instead, the best version of yourself is about how you react and cope with imminent situations that will unfold in your daily life. The Universe will continue expanding, the world will continue spinning, people will keep fighting for their own happiness in opposite directions, and you will continue having feelings and emotions—it's part of your nature. Therefore, keeping yourself together and your mind focused on yourself and your goals is imperative to face the impermanence of life.

Whether you continue doing what you are doing or decide to make a big change in your life, the only thing you will ever have is you and the way to face life. And it is this best version of yourself, the one that always wants to grow, expand and learn, the one you want to keep showing to yourself and the people around you.

Exercise – Identify Your Triggers

For the next week, be aware of your negative feelings; every day, pick one or two negative feelings you observe and write them down on paper. You can name them as you want, but try to be original.

Next to each feeling's name, identify the trigger, and write the experience, the word, and the moment that triggered that negative feeling. Then, at the end of the week, in a quiet place where you meditate or know you will not be disturbed, go to each one of the feelings and triggers and ask your intuition what the reason for that Samskara or impression is.

Finally, ask your intuition to take you to the moment, the place, and the event that stored the energy inside you, and write down the first voice that comes to your mind, the one of your intuition. You will know it is the right answer, you will identify a tone of truth, and you may perceive a physical reaction. If you don't detect the truth, it does not matter. The answer will come when the time is right to understand and not before. You only need to ask and listen; you don't need to force anything.

Chapter 12 – Creating New Habits

"When we shift out of a lower to a higher energy pattern, we create a protective shield on the energetic level, as it were, and we can no longer be psychically vulnerable to that other person."

- David R. Hawkins, Letting Go: The Pathway of Surrender -

Everything is Energy

Life goes on, and the earth will not stop spinning just because you have started meditating or discovered a new purpose and passion in life. Dharma will continue its way, unexpected things will still happen, and decisions will be hard to make. Change is uncomfortable, and for much that you heal, you will continue being a human being with a past, fears, hormones, and feelings.

For this reason, the purpose of this chapter is to consolidate all the things we have learned and create the ultimate set of tools to navigate life with a better posture, especially for moments of uncertainty and fear.

This chapter will be the one to keep in your pocket to remind you that despite everything, life and the Universe are in harmony, and there is no need to control it. Therefore, it is vital to raise your energy and keep it up in moments of doubt. The better you feel about the present and yourself, the more your decisions will be discerning.

I have talked about energy but haven't yet explained what that means. However, like many ideas in this book, it is more about how you feel and interact with the concept than a concrete theory or meaning. So, for example, if I asked your energy level, you would have an answer; you would start focusing your awareness on your thoughts, senses, and emotions and figure out how you feel.

Energy can be understood in many ways. One is like an internal force that tells you when you want to do something and how you want to do it. When your energy is low, leaving your bed in the morning is hard, and the willpower you put in for the rest of the day may be passive. Your attitude to embrace that day will fade, and if something doesn't change your feelings, many things will feel out of place. But other times, when your energy levels are high, you feel like you have the world in your hands and are unstoppable. Those days you go for a run, you finish the report waiting for days on your desk, and you finally paint the fence as you were told to ages ago.

Everything has energy, and energy controls everything. However, as energy is invisible and cannot be measured by our five senses, many skeptics don't believe that energy is part of the human experience and think it is pseudoscience or something created by a bunch of individuals singing Kumbaya. However, the good thing about energy is that it is a true reality whether or not you believe in it. If, for example, you do a little Google search, many of the most important scientists, thinkers, and philosophers of the world have spoken about energy, and not only the energy in regards to science and physics, but as the essence of life: Nikola Tesla, Aristotle, Thomas Edison, Friedrich Nietzsche, and Stephen W. Hawking.

Everything is transformed through energy, and energy can be measured at different levels of our existence. For example, in classical physics, we can measure energy as the amount of "work" required to move a certain weight for a determined distance: joules. In electromagnetism, weight is no longer crucial, and frequency becomes the main unit of measurement. In medical research to measure energy, for example, they used the SQUID magnetometer, which measures the tiny biomagnetic fields and can perceive those generated by humans and animals. If we go deeper into the scale of quantum mechanics, we can also measure the energy of any atoms or components in the Universe. We can measure the energy in everything: the energy emitted by the sun, the movement of the planets, the food you are eating, and the electrons of the atoms of a rock traveling in space. Everything vibrates at a certain frequency

You can feel the energy even when you don't have the equipment and cannot know the exact frequency; we were all born with this superpower. If something does not feel good, it feels negative. If it feels good, it feels positive. This superpower is available because our body communicates through energy as well. Our neurons, for example, use chemistry and electrical signals to communicate among themselves. These signals travel throughout our body to give information about how we feel and to take action. Some of these energetic impulses come from within our body to let us know we are sick, tired or happy, and others sensations come from the stimulation of the external world. For example, the anger you feel when someone hurts the person you love, and the sadness you feel when you see someone crying are feelings of empathy resulting from your mirror neurons' capability to simulate the actions and experiences of others in your brain. This example describes how your brain can transform energy, the ones of your brain, into feelings and sensations.

Similarly, you can feel you don't like a certain place or feel uncomfortable in certain streets or around certain people. That means that the frequency of those places and situations vibrates at a frequency you perceive is oddly different from what you are used to experiencing. It results from the tension between different frequencies, and it can be felt both ways, whether in lower or higher levels of energy compared to the situation. Sometimes, the instant reaction of our body can be extreme, so you feel stressed or anxious. Other times, they are subtle and can be described as a gut feeling; like you know something, but you don't know exactly how you know it.

There are other examples of how energy is felt. Think about when someone is staring at your back, and you look back because you felt something "calling" from behind. This situation also happens in the opposite way when you are staring at someone, that person turns and looks at you, and then you try to pretend you are not looking. It is like a form of subconscious communication that may result from our consciousness observing particles, as quantum physics explains in the double-slit experiment. The experiment shows that electrons change their behavior from energy to particles just by observing them. If you want to become more familiar with this, look for it. It is one of the most fascinating interrogates of our current civilization. The door to understanding how consciousness affects matter and how what we see may not be what is real.

Energy can also be manifested in our relationships with others, and they can mutate with time. For example, I used to hang out with a friend I loved; I still love him. We were inseparable for over a decade and used to have a blast together. He is one of the funniest people I know; it is almost impossible not to laugh after only two minutes of conversation. He is also very honest and sincere, a fundamental value we have lost in many relationships. However, as soon as I became more aware of my feelings and sensations, I started noticing that he often made me very uncomfortable.

As an experiment, I started to pay attention to my energy when we spoke or spent time together. It did not take long to realize that I felt irritated and angry every time we spoke. A simple five-minute conversation could ruin my entire day. As a result, I consciously decided to keep some distance. I knew it would benefit me and my state of mind. You understand by now that he was not entirely the cause of my pain; he was probably the trigger of my impressions and my interpretation of reality. However, I knew it was important at that time to be conscious of inner changes and the influence of the external world. Not only to know me better but also to have a state of mind to make better decisions.

Even when it seemed sad to decide to keep my distance from a friend, it was obvious that I started to feel lighter and more vibrant. Additionally, it was a liberating experience to understand how energy works and how to differentiate what is my energy and what is others' energy. It is vital for your well-being to understand that it is not always about you but also your surroundings and the people around you. But how do you explain a situation like this? Why does someone you love that much, that has been your sincere friend for many years, have the capability to trigger your negating feelings? And the answer is simple; both started vibrating at different frequencies, and the energy was no longer compatible.

This situation with my friend did not happen as suddenly as I thought. The situation started because I was going through a dramatic change in my life. I noticed he irritated me when I was experiencing the "point of no turning back" and an awakening to a new life. As the way I was interpreting the world was almost transforming completely, it was natural that we had less and less in common. I am sure he cannot explain yet what happened during that time. He probably never wondered or never will. Regardless, I will be here waiting to build a new friendship when our frequencies match again.

If you discern a little further, this may be why many friendships, long relationships, or marriages are over without apparent reason. Not simple fights or constant triggers destroy a relationship of 10, 20, or 30 years, nor is the idea that we never really know people or that there was no real love. Instead, what ends relationships is the constant change within us; our impermanence. Change that accumulates through time in our minds and hearts occasioning irreversible ruptures when we don't grow together with the other. They result from the unbearable tension of different energies that must continue their paths apart.

You are constantly moving in different ranges of frequencies, which can vary between periods, days of the year, or even moments of the day. Sometimes you start facing strong and repealing energies from your partner, friends, or family, ongoing situations that bring you anger or instability instead of bringing peace and love. In situations like this, people generally encounter two options: move away to keep growing apart or level themselves to the energy fields around them. Unfortunately, as we were never taught how to deal with situations like this, there was not a primary school class that teaches how to perceive and deal with energy, so normally the decisions of moving forward with your life or leveling your energy with others happen unconsciously. Only when you start better understanding your surroundings, yourself, and the energy around you do those decisions become conscious and under your control.

For our benefit, Dr. David R. Hawkins wrote a series of books you can study to go deeper into the understanding of frequencies, vibration and energy and the relationship with your consciousness. His research can be crucial for understanding your life and life itself. Furthermore, in the following pages, I will summarize all the practical tools we discussed and add new tools to maintain a high energy level. I call this tool kit *Energy Keepers*. They will help you to recuperate the energy in the present moment and connect with your inner voice in moments of doubt or despair; when your inner energy field feels low. Most of these energy keepers are very easy to implement, and the more you practice them, the more attuned to your real self you'll be. The real challenge here is to make them a habit.

Energy Keeper 1 – Positive Thinking

Positive thinking is one of the most important energy keepers. It resides in ourselves, it's free, and it's amazingly powerful. When I mean thoughts, I mean judgments, resentments and the mental invention of catastrophes. These types of thoughts, as we saw in the previous chapter, are translated by your body into feelings that are energy moving through your system, sometimes not very beneficial for your body, like the case of cortisol. When you change the judgment around your experiences, when you change it on a subconscious level, the real magic starts happening.

As we learned, problems are only in your mind, and it is the energy they produce within you that makes you feel something is actually happening. So, when your mind is taking you to a negative state, where you are a victim, you are not good enough, and where life is unfair and unpredictable, switch that thought and try to look for a tone of truth.

The tones of truth refer to thoughts that come from your soul and make you feel better instantaneously. However, it is important to pay a lot of attention before changing your thought and consider the chance to accept and understand the Universe unfolding before you, which may be better than you think. The tones of truth are not found by simply avoiding reality and repeating an affirmation that has no relation to yourself. Instead, finding the tone of truth is about learning from what you think and feel in the present moment. So, when judgment and negativity arrive in your system, do not simply avoid the thought and the feeling with it, but rather observe them and let them speak. Negative thoughts about the world, people, the government, your neighbors, and your coworkers tell you a lot about yourself—your fears, shame, and guilt. They are representations of the energy stored in your heart—impressions, or samskaras, that you can only really let go when you understand that it is not you real you speaking through them but years of toxic programming and limiting beliefs.

After you observe a negative thought and the discomfort of the feeling it brings, let your intuition travel to the first time you felt the same—Similar to the exercise you did when identifying your triggers. Ask your inner self how or when this thought, idea or belief was created. Whether you have an instant answer or not, remember that you are loved, smart, sovereign, and your life's creator. You are worthy of magic and deserve the life of your dreams. With this energy, connect to your heart and listen to what it says. Remember that your intuition, inner self or heart does not speak from fear or jealousy. So, what you hear when you are in absolute syntony with them, are the positive thoughts you need at that moment: encouragement, abundance, and wisdom. Loudly repeat all the thoughts you are hearing when tunning with your heart, at least three times, and let them sink in your mind.

Try to practice this in the present moment, right after you experience a negative thought or the thought followed by a trigger. That's the best way to create a new relationship with your thoughts, start reconfiguration the connections of your brain, and create new trends of thinking. If you don't have the space or the time to stop what you are doing to find the tone of truth right away, write down what happened and what you felt, and later that day or that week, try this exercise again.

Another way of identifying negative thoughts is by being aware of your words because words are no more than expressions of thought. When you start paying attention to what you say in random conversations, you will detect that not everything is positive or inspiring. Judgment, criticism, sarcasm, and jealousy are more frequent in our conversation than you imagine. Your words also work like a speaker that creates an infinite loop: you think about it, you say it, you hear it, your brain absorbs it again, and you think it again. Try to capture the attention of your words when speaking about others, even when you think you have the right to be upset because they reacted wrongly against you or were unfair to you. Then, practice the exercise I describe in the preview paragraph so you can find a new tone, the one of truth. Identify why you are so upset, think about when you felt this sensation the first time, and listen to what your heart wants to say.

If the answers are unclear when finding your tone of truth, try not to discuss the topic again in the next conversation. Talking negatively about a person or a situation will feed your ego more negativity instead of healing or changing your reality. And this recurrent attitude will bring more of the same and keep you attached to unhealthy energies. It is time to understand that nothing in your life is more important than your energy field and your well-being.

Energy Keeper 2 – Forgiveness and Compassion

Accepting the Universe is also accepting people, and people include the most important person—YOU. But unfortunately, most individuals, including us, are lost souls ruled by our egoic minds. Therefore, accepting others as they are, becomes one of the biggest challenges in life. To do so, we must understand that consciousness is a superpower only a few understand and master. And realize that most people walking on the earth today live in constant pain and suffering without acknowledging it and desperately looking for something without knowing what that is.

One of the biggest roots of their suffering is ignoring that they are responsible for their own lives, thoughts, and reactions; the only tool they have considered is to blame others for their disgrace. So most of them are out there pointing the finger at those responsible for their misery: ex-husbands, the opposite sex, unfair bosses, mean brothers, unthankful children, unfair government, terrorists, etc. And this is not more than the result of a civilization where victimhood is celebrated, and the warriors trying to excel in their lives are not always considered the heroes of the story but the problem to others' egos.

Like this victimhood program, there are many other limiting beliefs that a human needs to face that not only come from personal experience come from the whole society, which are programs harder to identify. Understanding that each person has to deal with their fights and the toxicity of a vicious world is the first step to compassion and the acceptance of others. Everyone wants to be happy, even when their egos are hidden from the truth. They are also looking for something, and they are also you.

So, the next time you meet someone you may don't like or agree with, or even worse, someone who attacks you or offends you, instead of judging, try to accept them first and love them as you love yourself. Observe the entire Dharma and the variables moving through millions of years of evolution for you to meet that person, and realize that being in the presence of that individual is an actual miracle of the Universe and therefore brings a lesson for you.

As we said before, it is no longer about forgiving you or forgiving others. It is about understanding that our automatic responses don't let us always make the best decisions or act properly in every situation. Your new life is more about understanding and cultivating compassion for people different from you, including accepting what you believe are their "flaws." People are, in fact, the best spiritual growth teachers you will ever have. So, learn how to grow with them and keep them in your heart as a reflection of you before ever judging or resetting them again.

Energy Keeper 3 – News, Social Media, and Movies

I was raised with the idea that being informed about what is happening in my country and the world is not only important, it is paramount. In my house, the world stopped when it was time for the news. My father didn't even let us speak during the headlines. Interrupting the headlines or the news was almost considered sacrilege. Similarly, my mother believes that a person's education level is proportional to the names of politicians they know, meaning that you are not well educated if you don't know who the Defense Ministry in our country was. Finally, other people still believe that political interest is proportional to the interest you have in your life. So if you don't care about politics, you don't care about your future and the future of those around you. Sometimes it feels like an obsession to watch or listen to the news as if whatever is said about the current president is the pinnacle of their life and existence.

My question for you: is this really useful in your life?

If your job requires you to be informed about the last president's tweet or the thousands of kids who died in the war in Ukraine last week, then yes, you must keep watching the news and screening social media. But if you don't need to watch or listen to the news for your job or to survive, stop watching the news. It won't hurt anybody, and you will start feeling better in a few days. It works like magic or better said: it is energy.

Starting today, carefully choose what you watch and who you follow on social media. Unfollow whatever and whoever brings negativity to your thoughts and your soul. It is a practical way to avoid feeding your ego with more hate, and it does not worth your time.

The best way to change your world and those around you is by keeping your energy up or upgrading your energy field. But this won't happen by hoping it to happen; this will only happen if you make the decisions and then act towards that transformation.

For those who have to watch the news as part of your work, please, pay attention to how you deal with it and do not take the bad news personally. Politicians are not doing what they are doing because life is unfair to you, and hopefully, terrorists are not attacking you and your family right now. You will not save the world by reposting and letting us know that there are egoic people committing atrocities. We all already know that. Rather, keep yourself informed practically and do not involve your feelings. Watch the news, understand how politics may affect your decision-making process, and act accordingly. As the media knows, people love watching bad news, so they primarily focus on those. They also push the agendas of those in power to manipulate the population's mood. So, try to be cleverer and stop playing the game of the media, a game your negative ego loves to play. It is not easy, and I know it. After five years of changing this habit, I still have the urge to post against tyranny and injustice. However, I know how to control my emotions and not feel pain anymore about situations I cannot control.

I know you don't want to be indifferent to the world, and for this reason, I am sharing three options: one option is to find your purpose and work for it; the second is to look at who in your family needs your spiritual support and be there; or the last one is to Google "Orphanage and Nursing Homes near me." And if you want to be informed, find scholars that inspired you or topics you are interested in —astronomy, Jungian psychology, quantum computing, Feng Shui, neurology, permaculture or movie making— and read related books and research papers. Millions of books and science magazines are waiting to be read and discovered. In this way, you can keep yourself up to speed about the events that are really supporting and changing the world. I assure you, any of these options is better for you and others than multiplying bad energy and fear around the planet.

I love watching movies and sometimes series, and I do it for two reasons, one is that I learn a lot from them, and two is mere entertainment with my family, friends and my partner. Movies and tv shows, however, also transmit energy, so it is important to decide what to watch as well consciously.

Understand, you don't have to watch everything out there, particularly regarding violence and horror. But this is especially true when you are trying to upgrade your life, and energy field, so you should cherish every single moment to allow it. Feeding your soul with more movies of hope and love may also be important in your transformation.

Yes, you don't have to be an extremist either; you can still join your friends to watch some movies, as I'm sure being around them also fills you with positivity. Just try to remember the brain is like a computer, and every little new thing it watches has the potential to be transformed into a new program, so being more critical about what you put in your brain is critical.

Energy Keeper 4 – Watch What You Eat

I spoke a little bit about food in chapter six, and we understood there is a strong connection between the digestive system and the brain. For example, strong emotions affect our digestion, and bad bacteria may tell our brains to crave sweets and fries. Also, we know some other harmful foods and habits can be related to cancer or diabetes.

Nevertheless, what we put into our bodies is hard to control sometimes, especially when we live in a civilization where unhealthy food, cigarettes and alcohol are widely accepted. Also, big corporations, governments and the media have not only defined what we can consume or not but constantly pushed propaganda and commercials to consume more regardless of the benefits to human health. They have been telling us that smoking is sexy, drinking is not bad, that pork is white meat and red meat in a burger is just $1.99.

However, others do not always need to tell us how to eat and what is good for us. Our body is sharing information with us constantly. Let's try to be honest: how do you feel after a burger, fries, and a coke? If you say to yourself, "it feels great, it fills me with energy," you might be either lying to yourself or not being present with your body. Being more aware of the sensations after eating certain foods is imperative for your physical and mental health and energy levels. Start today, compare the sensation of eating the burger versus the sensations after eating a natural smoothie, a portion of pineapple, steamed vegetables and low-fat chicken.

When you start paying attention to the sensations of your body after eating, really connecting to how you feel, it will be easy to recognize what makes you feel down or sick. When you give yourself a moment of discernment after or even before you eat, your brain will consciously learn what is good for your body; therefore, changing your diet will be easier daily. However, this exercise can also help you identify the lies in your mind and the tones it uses to speak to you. For example, if you think your body keeps choosing a drink of alcohol and fried cheese over a salad and mineral water, you would know it is your ego — your culture and your inner arrogance; or, as we learned before, it can be your gut bacteria.

Nevertheless, we need to do comprehensive research to know what is good for us while we get used to the voices of our bodies. But before you start this research regarding what to eat, I can briefly explain where to start: do not eat processed food. If what you are about to consume has been artificially processed or has artificially added products, it's not good; the more processes and artificial content there is in what you eat, the less healthy for you. Without trying to tell you to live off of lettuce and nuts, the chances to eat healthy when you eat non-processed foods are higher.

However, you don't need to stress about this or overthink it; the more conscious you are about your body, thoughts, life and decisions, the more you'll understand the kind of world you live in, so you won't be tricked by the system anymore. As a consequence, you will naturally look for better sources of information regarding what to eat because it's not necessarily all the things labeled as gluten-free, lactose-free, vegetarian, or vegan. You have all the knowledge of the Universe to be healthy in your body and in hand, your cellphone. For our benefit, we no longer live in the Middle Ages, where we did not have options at grocery stores.

Still, the bigger question here is not about knowing what to eat or not or what is good or bad for our gut. The real question is why we are still looking for excuses to harm our physical body, especially when we know that most things in excess: smoking, sugar, alcohol, and processed food, are harmful. But finding the answer in this instance is not about external resources. You are the only one with the answer because s something in deep in your mind that is telling you to pick what is not good. For example, I know exactly the moments of my life when I've been overweight and the reason behind them. Generally, it was when I passed through high anxiety and stress. I didn't know it then, but now I know that every burger, every French fry, and every glass of alcohol had a reason. I was interchanging a negative feeling or void in my heart by satiating the desire to eat.

When people know that behaviors like these are temporal, and they consciously know they will go away after they change the current situation, it may not be as harmful and will be fixed at some point. But when you don't know why you are in a vicious circle and keep gaining weight regardless of what you do, it's time to dig deeper and discover the real cause. Yes, it's excessive consumption of calories, but why are you letting your mind do that to you?

Food intake is a very complex topic and depends on many variables. However, I am calling your attention to be more aware of your eating and realize the importance of food as a vital energy source. You are the only one who can change to improve the relationship with what you eat. You are the ultimate person deciding what to put in your system, so feeding your body with the love you have for yourself is a good start.

Energy Keeper 5 – Watch Your Environments, Surroundings, and the People You are Sharing Your Time With

So far, we have talked about energy from your standpoint of view. You are the only one controlling your thoughts, what you let into your brain, and what you eat. But now, focus on the external world's energy, which is essential because we cannot directly control it.

People who master energies have the superpower of controlling the degree to which external energies affect them. Regardless of where they are, they won't get overwhelmed by their surroundings and won't absorb external energy as their own. People with high levels of consciousness and awareness will differentiate what is coming from the inside and from the outside world, whether from things or people. With this knowledge, they will easily filter what to keep for themselves and what should remain outside, therefore not taking anything personally. When people are not at this level of controlling how energies affect them, I recommend identifying what put you down and putting yourself far from those environments.

Going back to my friend's example, I started to identify that I was having a normal day and felt full of energy on several occasions, but I started to feel charged, tense, and upset when I was sharing time with him. Initially, it was difficult to identify what made me feel drained, but with time and more attention to my thoughts, feelings and triggers, I started to better comprehend how other people react and behave. In this case, I understood that my friend takes random comments personally, which triggered his impressions or samskaras. This release of contained negative energy is absorbed by people around him, in this case, by his friend. For this reason, when in direct contact with certain people, some get upset for no apparent reason.

When you start identifying when negativity does not rise from you but from others, your system will filter it easier and release the inner tension. With time, your days won't be affected anymore by the impressions or reactions of others. Remember, the first step is to be aware; after that, letting go and releasing negative energies is easier.

You know, when you are in a positive state or when you are in a negative state; it is one of your human superpowers, and you should benefit from that wisdom. So, start paying attention whenever you feel low energy and start identifying what is draining it. Please write in your journal what happens in your system, when it is happing, and where. Little by little, you will start discovering patterns and identifying people or places consuming your energy. Do not pay much attention to whatever happens after 4 p.m.—at that time, most people have consumed all their fuel and have less control over their emotions; by design, people are more irritable.

Energy Keeper 6 – Life Acceptance

Love your life with all its flaws and imperfections, always remembering that acceptance is not apathy. Acceptance is about understanding that the external world we were born in is still filled with fear and won't change during our lifetime. Change can only be found in the extent of the change you can make within yourself.

I know there are difficult situations to accept in life, like death. Death is particularly tough because our brains have been programmed to perceive death as bad and painful. In most cultures, dying is something to be extremely afraid of because it has a deeply negative connotation. This affirmation does not mean that death should be positively perceived. I'm trying to say that we need to change our relationship with death to start accepting it as part of the natural course of life. We will all die; your body and the body of the people you love won't be on earth for several years. I know it's hard to think about it, but dying isn't something we can change or deny. The only thing we can do is change the extreme fear and the relationship with it.

Death is, in fact, one of the reasons we leave our bed every morning and go to work. Survival is the ultimate instinctive motive to keep our lives running. It is almost impossible to imagine how life would be if death didn't exist. This world wouldn't be similar to what it is because most things we love probably would not exist, and the experience would differ from what we all feel today. I could even affirm that the recurrent fight against death structured our way of living and civilization.

When someone you love dies, the only real thing that is gone is their physical body and the possibility of sharing new moments with them again. However, 'who' they are can never die. The concept of who they are will be part of your history forever and remain in your memory until you, as well, leave this reality. All the good things you learned about them and your experience with them are already part of who you are, your heart, your heart and your impressions.

Something similar happens to the other difficult situations we must face — being abandoned by someone we love, having a disease, suffering bankruptcy, and being fired from our job. But, after the anger and the mourning, accepting it and learning from it is the wiser path. Otherwise, it is choosing to live hell on earth and contempt the only possibility to enjoy life with everything it brings. We cannot control everything, plus the idea of control also fills your system with additional tension because it knows that you cannot control the entire Universe.

Energy Keeper 7 – Connect with the Now

As mentioned several times in the book, being in the now can be one of the most important tools for keeping your energy up. It does not only keep your energy high, but it also acts as an energy charger, a supercharger. Of course, you already know some techniques to bring you to the present moment, but I want to share a fun one with you.

The next time you are in your mind, overthinking and preoccupied, play your favorite song—ideally your favorite happy song—and dance to it. Bring to the now the little energy you have and dance to that song as if you were the best dancer in the world, as if every movement of your body was magnificent, which it is. You are a miracle, remember? Be aware of the movements, breathing, and changes in your heart rate. Just observe. Sing; sing loud as if you were the best singer in the world. Feel the words and pay attention to the energy they bring. You will see how in a matter of seconds, you feel better.

If you don't have a favorite song, I can lend you one of mine. It's not my favorite song, but it is the one I like dancing to: "I Miss You" by the Rolling Stones—the only condition is that you have to dance like Mick Jagger for the magic to happen. Google 'Mick Jagger dancing,' and you'll see why.

When you do this, you bring all your senses to the present moment and give yourself a new opportunity to understand that nothing is happening and you are fine. You can play a song written three decades ago and dance to it with happy movements— seriously, what else can you ask for in life? You can use this method anytime you feel you need to come back to yourself again.

If you think this is just a way to avoid problems, you are also right. Most problems do not exist. They are just inventions of your mind because most things haven't happened yet. And if something has already happened, there is little you can do about it rather than accept it and move on with the best energy you can have.

Next time you feel that you are hitting rock bottom, instead of having a drink, eating a bucket of ice cream, and watching something meaningless, try the Jagger Method, and you will see the difference. Your mind will be clearer to decide better what to do next. It may be the ice cream, but you will also be more ready to breathe, meditate, and observe your thoughts and feelings. The idea of returning to the now is to get out of your head to stop listening to your ego's theories or keep sinking.

Energy Keeper 8 – You are Your Best friend

In chapter eight, we spoke about the conversations you have with yourself and how to change those thoughts. There is no justification for you to have negative beliefs and thoughts about yourself moving forward. The only person that has an obligation to love you is you and no one else. Loving ourselves should be the sole purpose of every human being; still, it is not up to me to decide what everyone's purpose is.

Love yourself, and every time you are about to do something you are unsure about, ask your real self if you would recommend this to the person you love the most or your best friend. The answer should come easily come from your soul.

Energy Keeper 9 - Find an Inspiration, a Coach, a Mentor

Some people looking to start a personal or spiritual growth process and become a better version of themselves constantly get lost in their thoughts, programs, their past stories, fears, and negativity, so seeing the light within is very hard. For this reason, it is extremely important to find external help. When people believe they can do all the transformational work alone, and they do not understand how their ego and the subconscious mind work, they chose the path of auto-sabotage and victimhood.

Probably you have unconsciously picked your superheroes—someone to inspire you regardless, to listen to or read when you are not in the best moment. For example, our parents or the people who raised us are our primary superheroes when we are kids. They are always there for shelter. Even sometimes, when we are adults, they are still there to save us.

In my case, other superheroes also came along the way: Carl Sagan, the Dalai Lama, Simon Sinek, and Michael Singer are examples of other inspirations, one for every moment of my life. They have always been there to teach me about the Universe, compassion, leadership, and spirituality. You wouldn't believe me if I told you I had the opportunity to meet all of them except for Carl Sagan, who died when I was still a teenager in 1996. The Dalai Lama went to Colombia in 2006, and I attended his talk on a weekday afternoon. I met Simon Sinek in New York City in 2015 when I was selected to participate in one of his private workshops; he signed my book, and we took a selfie together. I visited Michael Singer at his meditation center in 2017, where we meditated and chanted together. I followed them for years before meeting them. I read their books and listened to their talks. Today, I know that the force of the Universe that made me meet them was in me. After all, I'm the creator of my own life.

If you do not recognize any superhero, you may intentionally look for influencers who are linked to the topics you are more passionate about and even your purpose. For example, someone you want to inspire you in the long run, you want to learn from, and someone you feel you want to become — a role model.

However, even when their inspiration is important to guide us, many of these superheroes remain in the realm of dreams. They probably have little things in common with you, and the presence they may share with you is ephemeral. For this reason, finding a mentor or a coach from the real world is very important; someone who has personally passed through the path of self-growth, who is awakened and understands love and kindness. Your friends and family are perfectly fine to support you and help you forget your problems, but many people are still on the victim's side of their ego. And they will unintentionally feed your fears and insecurities. If you are looking for real transformation, you need someone who helps you become the superhero others may need. Many coaches, healers, meditation teachers, and yoga teachers await you. We all want to make a difference in the world.

Energy Keeper 10 - Starting Your Day as Best as You Can

Are you starting your day grumpy, hating the sound of the alarm, complaining about getting up, and hating that it is time to go to the office? Be attentive because this tells you much about how you are embracing your life. Additionally, the first moments of the day set the tone for the rest of the day; this energy is what you will be carrying and sharing with others. So, instead of a moment of objection or hatred, change the habit and try to be grateful. Life is giving you a new day and an opportunity to grow, experiment, learn, fail, love, and sing. This day can be exactly the day that everything changes and will bring the opportunity you were expecting. Still, your overthinker mind is clouded by negativity, and you may not even see it.

If you can work on your passion and purpose first thing in the morning, do it and make that your 6 a.m. or 7 a.m. appointment. I also recommend working out and meditating afterward; it is one of the best things you can do before starting your day. You will have endorphins running within your system and feel fabulous the rest of the day. If you cannot do it for whatever excuse of your ego, such as "I cannot wake up early" or "I am not a morning person," try to find something else; for example, time for breakfast with your family, coffee with your spouse, walking your dog, yoga, a cold shower, singing, dancing, screaming out of the window and thanking the Universe. Find the first thing in the morning for you, for your soul—not for your boss, your job, or anyone else, but for you.

Exercise – Create Your Own Habits

It is hard to change all your bad habits in a week or a month, but it is possible to do it gradually. You only need to have a powerful reason, a goal, and to know it is possible to make it. Just believing, in this case, is not enough; you need to know — to be certain. Creating new habits is the fourth step of The Matryoshka Method, Reinvent Yourself.

Create a list of all the things you want to change; take the 10 Energy Keepers for inspiration and chapter six, where you qualified all of the aspects of your life. Then, start implementing the easiest changes the first week, add another the second or the third week, and so on. I assure you that you'll feel lighter in a month, and the people around you will notice the difference.

Remember, we are not only talking about getting up at 5 a.m. every morning so you can run for an hour. We are talking about little changes to maintain your energy, eating less processed food, drinking more alkaline water, changing your negative thoughts, judging people less, praying when you wake up, remembering that you love yourself, watching less empty TV, reducing your time on social media, etc. Those are very easy to do; you only need to start now.

You can manually create a calendar on a sheet of paper to start tracking the changes you will implement. Add the new habit you want to implement every week, keeping the previous ones for constancy. After a month of new habits, keep them for at least two more months, and only include a new set of habits in the 4th month. Through this, you ensure the first set of habits already became habits for good, and your brain pathways have changed properly. Keeping this calendar will also help you start leveling up the natural dopamine intake that your system needs.

Habits Calendar							
Week 1	1	2	3	4	5	6	7
Running 3 times a week	• Running		• Running		• Running		
Week 2	8	9	10	11	12	13	14
Meditate every day for 20 minutes	• Running • Meditate	• Meditate	• Running • Meditate	• Meditate	• Running • Meditate	• Meditate	• Meditate
Week 3	15	16	17	18	19	20	21
Read three times a week my favorite book	• Running • Meditate	• Meditate • Reading	• Running • Meditate	• Meditate • Reading	• Running • Meditate	• Meditate • Reading	• Meditate
Week 4	22	23	24	25	26	27	28
Work every morning on my new project	• Running • Meditate • NewProyect	• Meditate • Reading • NewProyect	• Running • Meditate • NewProyect	• Meditate • Reading • NewProyect	• Running • Meditate • NewProyect	• Meditate • Reading • NewProyect	• Meditate • NewProyect

Figure 5 – Example of a habits calendar

Chapter 13 – Plan Your New Career

"The neural processes underlying that which we call creativity have nothing to do with rationality. That is to say, if we look at how the brain generates creativity, we will see that it is not a rational process at all; creativity is not born out of reasoning."

- Rodolfo Llinas-

So far, you have discovered many new things about yourself, life, and the universe, and eventually, you started feeling ready to move on and plan your professional future. You also understood that you don't need to spend most of your life in places you dislike and situations that discomfort your soul. However, it's also important to be conscious that most situations you feel bad about are not, in fact, bad; they are programs you learned from modern civilization or inventions fed by the pessimistic ego. For example, knowing that others have more cars, houses, money, salary, trips, and diplomas can make you feel like you are always behind. However, this does not mean that they are happier or that you have or be all of those things to feel successful in life. The reality is that the only thing you need more in your life is consciousness and creativity.

So far, you have completed 10 out of 12 steps of the Matryoshka Method, the necessary process before you make your final decision to stay or not to stay in your current job. Without all these steps to better understand who you are and what you want in life, you would probably feel as you felt before reading this book and for the rest of your life. Now you know, for example, that it is your responsibility to stop making decisions based on what you were told and what others do or think. You comprehend that happiness and peace are not sensations that just arrived from the sky or will be available the day you win the lottery. Finding happiness and peace in your life is a conscious work of your soul you must do with love and commitment.

At the end of this chapter, you will use what I call the *Job Decision Model* to gather your discoveries and easily visualize everything you have understood so far, facilitating the decision-making process. More than a rational process, it is a tool to assemble all that has been revealed to enhance your creativity. Please try not to share any thoughts about your decisions with anybody yet. Additional variables should be considered before deciding and moving forward with communicating.

Knowing what and who you are is essential before moving forward. You have probably found that the situations you thought you disliked about your job have a different explanation or cause.

You may have confirmed that you are passionate about what you do, and your main issues are outside the office because you don't have an equilibrated life; other aspects need more attention and make you feel continuously stressed and anxious. Maybe you realized that you had nothing in common with your place of work, and it is critical enough to consider a change of job or, better, a new career. The next step is to discern the different scenarios and see how your intuition responds.

There are only three options regarding a job decision: stay exactly where you are, change the situation, or leave it. Whatever you decide to do, you need to be at peace with that decision, and the only way to find peace is when you do it from the heart. This statement means that the decision is aligned with your values, your purpose, and your passion, and therefore, the trust in yourself.

In chapter five, we discussed how you decided on your career and why you have the job you have today. In that chapter, you discovered what type of person you were: the type that lives life expecting destiny to put opportunities in your way or who consciously looks to be where one wants to be. If you found out that you are the type of person number one, who is waiting for things to happen, I want you to acknowledge that today, you will become the type of person who makes life happens.

You are only certain about having this life, and the present moment is where the relationship with that life happens and the only opportunity you have to make things right. So it is your decision how you want to treat this opportunity to live. Do you want to continue to let life happen to you, or are you ready to look after the universe's abundance?

If living were statistically proven, we would use probability and models to determine what to do. But as life is just a manifestation of what you do with it, we only have the present moment to do the best and hope for the better: cause and effect. And the only real measure you have of your life is what your soul tells you through your intuition. So, before moving forward, try to connect to the feelings deeply, you are about to experience when imagining three possible futures: Keep the Job You Have, Change Your Current Situation, or Leaving Your Job. That gut feeling of each one of the scenarios is the most important measurement you have of your future. I strongly recommend practicing meditation or breathing exercises before you move on in this chapter.

Decision #1 – Keep the Job You Have

If you stay in your current job, whether you are a *Visionary Follower*, a *Trader of the Real* or *a Caged Dreamer*, try to imagine the best possible outcome of your future when answering the following questions.

- How does it feel to continue in the same job for a year, five, or ten years?
- Do you feel you are going to be living your values?

- Do you feel like you can stop experiencing whatever you don't like?
- Are you following your passion and living your purpose?

If the answer is yes for all of them and your heart tells you, "This is what I want to do for the rest of my life," your answer may be as simple as *staying*. You now have the tools to make your life lighter. All you have learned in this book can help you have the life of your dreams regardless of what you do.

Remember, you can live your passion and purpose from the workspace even when not 100% aligned. For example, suppose your purpose is related to helping people to improve their work-life balance. In that case, you can do that from your office — whether supporting your boss, helping your co-workers, understanding your subordinates, or listening to your clients.

If your bigger issue at the office is the amount of work and the anxiety, you can start a more frequent meditation practice and mindfulness every day at the office. You may even invite your team to practice meditation instead of gossiping in the hallway. This practice will help you be more efficient, decrease the stress level at the office, and stimulate your team's serotonin and oxytocin levels.

If your problems are outside the office and are more related to the lack of balance, you can pursue other goals and personal projects. For example, working on your health, family, and community will help you feel better about yourself and your life.

You can also start gradually changing your habits and increasing your energetic field.

If you decide to stay, never stop being conscious of your actions and feelings. For example, if your heart does not feel happy about your job, you may be listening to your fearful mind's excuses. It may be your ego telling you that you will not make it or that you are destined to fail. You can silence that part of you holding you back and start listening to whatever your soul desires. Those dreams in your mind are achievable. Don't ever forget that.

Finally, remember time does not exist and is only a construct of your mind. The now is the only door to step into the future you have always dreamed about, and the now is the only place to find happiness.

Decision #2 – Change Your Current Situation

You probably realized that the things which make you anxious are not necessarily for working for a firm or a corporation. Instead, your discouragement more likely comes from certain people, projects, and specific situations: you may not belong to a tribe within your organization, your boss does not appreciate your work, the area you are working in is not the one you like, or you may be traveling so much, that you are tired of sacrificing time with your family.

Regardless, as you are the ultimate person responsible for your career and life, it's time to act and stop being the victim of the circumstances. It's time to speak up and rip apart the conditions you are unwilling to accept.

B Before you take any actions to change your current situation, have an honest conversation with yourself and ask why is the real reason you don't feel happy and why you are deciding to stay in a discomfort zone. This inner conversation is important because, in most places, you will find issues—tough projects, people you don't get along with, overtime, and traveling. I want you to double-check your psyche and scan if other unconscious beliefs come to the surface; your lack of purpose or something additional related to your human nature is the real reason for your discomfort.

Few things should discourage you if you are passionate about something and really happy doing a certain job. For this reason, it is so important to ask yourself twice before moving your life around and find the tones of truth.

Whatever you decide to do next, keep in mind what you learn in the previous chapter; everything is energy. And as we were never taught how to identify and control energy, most people don't know which is their vibration. However, that doesn't prevent you from vibrating in a specific frequency of thoughts and feelings. The frequency that you are projecting to the world around you. For example, when you don't trust yourself, you project that onto others. When you don't trust others, you unconsciously project that onto them. So, if you want to demand changes in the workplace— to your boss, human resources, yourself, your soul, or your intuition—you need to be 100% aligned with what you are requesting. If you think you "might" feel better with a promotion, a change of location or a new project, you will not get it just by requesting it; it would help if you were 100% sure that your request is what you want and mean it. In other words, your values, purpose, and passion must be on the same page to manifest what you want. If you think deeper, good sellers and leaders are good only because they know what they are selling. In this case, you are selling yourself.

Dealing with people is vital for the next stage of your transformation. As we learned in the previous chapter, your relationship with others depends on your relationship with yourself. When you work on your confidence, you will be ready to move forward, decide, speak up, and take your career and life to the next phase. You will always reach a better stage when you are certain about what you want and who you really are.

One way to measure your confidence is to ask yourself if you care what others think about you. If you are currently deciding based on what your boss, friends, spouse, or mother will think, you haven't connected to your inner warrior, sovereignty, and self-love. You may not be valuing your deeper desires to fight for them, or you may not even know what you want from your life, so you need others' approval. Finally, you may not understand that you deserve the life you want no matter what others believe.

When you are conscious of what you want, and your values, purpose, and passion align, there is no room for hesitation or self-doubt. Of course, this statement isn't to say that you should ignore the people around and that will be affected by your decisions. But if you set your priorities right and consider your family's and loved ones' well-being, you only need to commit to your decisions no matter what. In other words, it is time to consider first what your soul desires and what you want in life.

Get ready to request others and the universe for whatever you know is the best in your current situation. You don't need to do any analytical work, learn something new or ask permission; you only need to fill your heart with courage to make things happen. When you are sure, you don't need to wait for an extra thing to happen or to find a new excuse. However, be thankful if you still feel insecure about moving forward and changing the current situation. This is just a sign, something you must revise inside you that needs to be understood and aligned. Whatever it is, face it, discern the opportunities and take action. If you want to change something it must happen and must come from you. Waiting on your desk for the miracle to happen is nothing more than procrastination.

Also, consider the reality that you can be mistaken, and what you are asking for is not what you wanted or won't bring the result your expected. Life is about taking massive imperfect actions toward your goals and desires. And even when you can see today why it is resulting differently from what you expected, life will give the answer, and you will connect the dots and realize that everything in life happens for a reason.

Every time you need to reevaluate your decisions, go back to your mind maps of passion and purpose, and remember that being scared does not mean it is not the right path. On the contrary, that feeling sometimes means excitement for future changes and transformation.

Decision #3 – Leaving Your Job

When you are positive that keeping your job and changing your current situation is not enough to find the joy and the happiness you are looking for, every day you spend in that job is a day you are living against yourself and betraying your value. If you are a *Trader of the Real*, at least you are not making your life a nightmare, and your energy level can be neutral, even if it's not the life you always dreamed of you. However, if you are in the *Caged Dreamers* group and don't have a specific plan of action to change the game, it's time to act and encourage yourself to serious movements toward your goals. In this scenario, you are at your lowest energy level possible, a victim of your work, and not in alignment with your values and purpose.

If you are a *Caged Dreamer*, you have a list of 100 reasons why you are keeping your job that can sound like this.

- You think there is only one place where you can earn that much money.

- You believe you have been doing the same job for so long that moving to another position is impossible.
- You think whatever you want to do requires a new diploma, and you don't have time or money.
- You have a lot of debt, so leaving a good job is irresponsible.

I'm not saying these reasons are false, but these "excuses" are thoughts and conversations you have with yourself, feeding your doubts and hesitation. Your ego is in fact excluding thousands of opportunities in the universe. If you don't decide and act now, years will pass, and you will likely be unsatisfied with your job until retirement. And only then will you know you had a chance to reinvent your life today.

Mr. Ego will always see changes as challenging and impossible, so we often decide to stay where we are. This is why, fighting our ego is probably the most complicated battle we will ever have: or better said, fighting our ego is the only real battle we have in our lives. As we know, Mr. ego, or unknowing what is hidden behind, limits you from pursuing your goals and dreams and taking the risk to move forward. That is the entity that fills you with anger, jealousy, and fear. That part of you that does not let you see your real self and listen to your intuition.

I thought that if I quit my job to get my master's, I would finally get the job I wanted. And that hasn't happened. Additionally, the second time I left the firm, I had to move out of the United States and leave the life I had behind—one of the most difficult decisions of my life. Today, I haven't achieved all of the things my ego wants. However, all the decisions were made from the bottom of my heart, a place where there is no space for regrets or resentment. On the contrary, they have brought unexpected and magnificent manifestations in my life, and sometimes not what my ego wants but what my soul desires, which sometimes are hard to understand rationally.

Before moving forward:
- Return to every possible decision #1, #2 and #3.
- Connect to the sensations and your intuition.
- Listen to your future self telling what is best for you.
- Remind yourself to trust you.

Planning the Separation and Finding a New Job

If your decision so far leans towards leaving your job. You have two options here: first, set a date, quit, and start looking for another job or setting up your business; or two, try to do your current job while looking for other options. You are the only one who can define the best option for you. I've done both, and both have worked just fine, and I see both options working with my clients. Many of them work with me when they are unemployed, and their entire panorama changes in a matter of weeks or months. This decision depends on your current situation and the specific needs you have. There are no rules.

Before you start looking for a job, you should have at least a set of three things defined: your job dislikes, your values, your passion, and your purpose. When you don't have these defined, you will randomly shoot until you find the highest bidder. As a result, you will send resumes for a random job you may be qualified for to companies you don't even know and probably end up stuck in a very similar situation as you are right now.

If you still feel lost on your decision, go back to chapter five to reconsider your values and chapter nine to reconsider your purpose and passion. But also remember that you can change how you see the world in the future, and nothing is written in stone. You, as well as your human nature, are impermanent; we all are in constant change. So don't commit the same "mistakes" as before, believing that you must follow a certain path because you committed to it years ago, and it is too late for a change. I use quotation marks because there are no mistakes in life for two simple reasons: first, you have lived amazing experiences, you have built a great network and grown immensely; second, all the situations you have experienced as of today have taught you everything you need to move forward. Everything in your life happens for a reason, and you are where you have to be.

Now that you know it is time to move and better understand what you want, imagine the work of your dreams; only focus on your job this time. You can be as rational or irrational as your brain allows but try to think outside the box, dream bigger, and be creative. Imagine when you start working, the commute (if any), your team, your duties, and your responsibilities. How do you feel about your job? How much money are you making, and for what? How many vacations, sick days, and bonuses will you get?

If whatever you imagine seems normal and does not scare you, you need to try harder. Every dream that comes true starts with a thought. Thoughts are limitless, so don't be so conformist as to think you will get 15% of your current salary, five more vacation days, and a bonus.

If you are over 50, do not let your age scare you. Many success stories started after 50, and putting a real dream into reality does not need to take decades; it can be done within months. If you are over 50 and haven't saved money or will not get retirement, you have nothing to lose. But if you don't try to do something new with your life that makes you happier, you have everything to lose: the option to be happy with what you do.

I also understand there is a limited demand for employment everywhere, especially in third-world countries. But you have the right to say that it is hard to find a job only when you have sent over 200 applications, letters, or resumes to the companies you would like to work for—only the ones you are sure you want to work for. So do not quit before starting the search; prove to the rest of the world and your ego they are wrong, and you could get a job not two times better but ten times better than what you have.

For example, go to LinkedIn; if you don't have an account, open one. Search for jobs in a specific city, the city you dream of living in, or the city you always wanted to visit and look for job offers with words related to your job or your passion. You will be impressed by the number of opportunities you can find. Of course, you don't need to limit yourself to LinkedIn; each country has its favorite job search pages.

If you are too scared of leaving your job because you need to pay your bills, again, don't limit yourself—plan. For example, allow yourself to save what you need to live for a year. If you make a certain amount a month, try to live with half of it. Then, invest and save the other half. We are talking about only one year of savings that can liberate your work for at least another year. Investing in yourself can be the most important investment you would ever make. You will only understand the magic behind a full year of planning your future, life, and happiness until you do it.

If you think your new career requires a new diploma, think twice about why you want to study. Remember discussing how you could be as prepared as a Georgetown student? Well, I'm serious. Sometimes, master's degrees, especially MBAs, are very generic. They are not specific, and the real reason behind the master's is to increase your networking or gain the credential. But consider that having the credential doesn't guarantee your desired job; only you can.

Start exploring what you want by studying and becoming a master in the topic before you decide to pay thousands of dollars for a diploma or a certificate. You are the only person who needs to be sure that you are an expert on something. Plus, all the world's knowledge is on your computer, through the Internet.

For example, when I decided to pursue my Executive MBA, I was looking for an excuse to leave the city and the job I didn't like, move abroad and learn a third language. I did it more because all those things sounded exciting and were part of my inner child's dreams. So, I recommend that if you want to get a new diploma, go for it, but do it for reasons additional to finding a better o a different job. Please do it for the passion you have for the topic and the experience of going back to school.

Starting a New Business

Starting a new business may sound like the best option for you, not simply switching jobs. You probably concluded that it's impossible to follow your values, passion, and purpose by being an employee and following the same career. If you are leaning toward this decision, I congratulate you. Starting a new business can be the most challenging decision ever, especially when it is believed that 90% of startups fail. However, the difference between a normal startup and your startup is that you have a real purpose or are on the path to finding it. Starting a new business also has the power to support the construction of the best version of yourself. The empowerment, healing, and confidence a personal venture builds are unimaginable.

Many startups and small businesses are founded to create a business that helps with retirement because people get tired of the 9 to 5 job or the 9 to "whenever" job, like in a big consulting firm. Even when many successful businesses exist only to make money and not for the passion of it, people get easily bored, feel more stressed and get tired before it breaks even. When you are not aligned with your purpose, your passion, your values, and therefore your soul is harder to find people that believe in what you believe. But, when it is a cause you believe in and feel passionate about, you have more options to be in the 10% that are successful. Passion can drive success in a more powerful way than just money.

You can also be independent in other ways. For example, many online modalities exist for people to make a living. This way, you don't need to limit your life to your neighborhood, city, or country—you have the Internet, and therefore, you have access to the entire world.

Searching for a new passion and career taught me that many businesses run only online. Many require little investment, whether for training or a software license to run it. After that, you can make money from the comfort of your home or a beach in Bali. The founders of the businesses will teach you techniques; they will give you scripts you need for selling and even train you in their software.

I have seen the following types of businesses in this modality: marketing and media manager, realtor, freelance bloggers and writers, small and medium businesses consultant, teachers, therapists and counselors, goods and services sellers, drop shipping, and traders. Some ensure you make $10,000 monthly to make more than $100,000 yearly if you work hard. And you won't even work more than 40 hours a week; some guarantee you don't have to work more than 20. If your real purpose, value, and passion align with what I just said, then you don't have an excuse now other than finding the proper coach and expert to teach you and help you create your business. Don't limit your job or your passion to the walls of a corporation; there are plenty of opportunities out there to be created aligned with your real self.

We live in the best time to be independent, whether as the founder of an idea, a movement, or a community. We understand we have the means to find all the information we need to move on. We only need to start working on it; the possibilities are infinite. The Internet gives you access to finding anything you want, wherever you want: a job, a scholarship, new skills, new clients.

Some people believe there is an overflow of services, coaches, consultants and online sellers, and this is true. I will not deny that online businesses worldwide have increased immensely, especially after the 2020 global restrictions. But this doesn't mean that there are no opportunities for you. Maybe, this only means more people is looking for good and services online. I am sure it is time to look directly into the eyes of the future and realize that this is the new world, and probably we are in the exact moment to establish that online business.

When starting their business, my clients have had the same questions and doubts, but soon they get surprised when they started seeing the number of people interested in their services. Most of the time, they get clients faster and way more than I do. You need to understand that you are not necessarily competing with Harvard, Tony Robins or Jeff Bezos. The people looking for you will need your specific knowledge, your services, your talent, and your unique energy.

Exercise – The Job Decision Model

This framework will help you visualize all the work done so far and start planning your next steps. Go to the following link to download the model in a spreadsheet to easily complete the blanks. You can also print it. Here there some tips for completing it.

Link: https://6h15.short.gy/DecisionModel

Job Decision Model

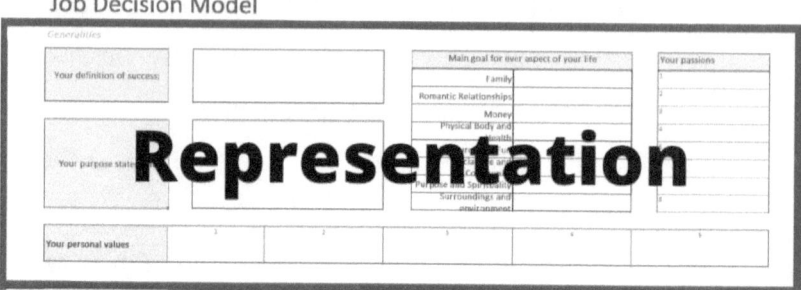

Figure 6 – Job Decision Model Representation

Your definition of success: Write down the definition of success you did in chapter seven.

Your purpose statement: Write down the purpose statement you defined in chapter nine. It does not have to be exact, and you can work with the ideas you have so far.

Main goal for every aspect of your life: Describe in a few words what you want to do for each one of the aspects of your life. You worked on this in chapter six.

Your passions: List what you love to do; it does not matter if it is unrelated to your ideal work. Creativity starts to rise when you see what you love from another perspective.

Your personal values: Go back to the exercise in chapter five. Where you understood better your human nature and defined your values, and write them here.

Professional goals/ ideal job: Identify the main characteristics of your dream job and what you expect from it. What does it need to change to experience a healthy

Decision: Remember, in this chapter, we reviewed your three options when you feel unhappy in your job: stay, change the situation or leave it. Pick the one you want from the bottom of your heart.

Activities: Activities are what you need to do to make that professional goal feasible and have to be concrete. For example, if you need a certification, the activity may not be to get the certification but to study for it. Add also a driver or a performance indicator, something you can measure. For example, in the "study for the certification," the driver would be the number of hours you will invest in this task per day or month. Finally, complete the deadline with the date you want to complete the specific activity. Don't think too much; try to go with whatever your intuition tells you.

Here are other examples of activities and drivers; the idea is to go deeper into the steps needed to achieve a goal, not only the endpoint.

Activity	Driver
Find a master's degree and make a list of the top 5	Research universities 10 hours per week for two months.
Save $20,000 to open the consulting boutique office	Save $1,000 every month and move to a cheaper apartment.
Improve my French	Study one hour every day for the next three months

Change my current position within the organization	Create a business case and talk to human resources or my supervisors about the case.
Find a new corporation to apply for	Research one hour daily, and apply to 50 different positions in the next two months.

Write as many activities as you want, even the ones you can start doing today. Also, for activities you will probably accomplish in a long time, you can still start making efforts towards them. However, you don't need to write down those activities and their drivers; you can only visualize them. And as soon as you can start working on them, include them in the list. This strategy is important so you don't overwhelm yourself with all you have to do, and it will help you organize your days and weeks without oversaturating your mind. Deep down in your heart, you know where you want to go, so you don't have to write everything you think you may be doing in a year.

Exercise –Brainstorm about your own business.

If you decide to leave your job and your career for good, and you want to start a new business and share your creation and knowledge with the world, use the *Job Decision Model* to brainstorm about your business. In the Activity or Goal section, start writing down ideas for your new business, considering all the variables of the model - purpose and what you want to say to the world.

Chapter 14 – Just Do It

"People tend to burden themselves with so many choices. But, in the end, you can throw it all away and just make one basic, underlying decision: Do you want to be happy, or do you not want to be happy? It's really that simple. Once you make that choice, your path through life becomes totally clear."

- Michael A. Singer, The Untethered Soul -

Overthinking, fear and procrastination

You are already at the starting point of making your goals a reality. When you have your purpose, passion, and values with you, there is nothing else you need to keep moving forward. However, our ego and what is behind it will always find an excuse not to do things and continue procrastinating and overthinking.

Procrastinating, however, is not always bad or the end of the world. It can be your unconscious mind telling you something. Maybe you don't feel ready, or there may be something you have not yet understood from your soul, so it is easy to get lost and forget our true path. Therefore, it is important to learn how to read your procrastination. Every time you postpone something for the next day, the next month or the next year, try to identify why. Be honest with yourself and look for the real reasons holding you back. When you are in alignment with your soul, nothing should stop you from your goals and the life of your dreams.

As you know by now, fear is always a reason you don't make decisions and move forward. The fear, particularly the one you are unaware of, can be your biggest enemy. If I could tell you that I traveled to the future, saw all your dreams becoming a reality, and the only thing you had to do was complete each planned activity, I'm sure you would do it without hesitation. It is normal to feel scared at a certain point, but when your fears become bigger than your dreams, it's no longer harmless and will block your life immensely.

From today, you will reprogram your relationship with fear. Instead of calling that sensation "fear" or something along those lines, you will start calling it "excitement" because going after your dreams should not feel dark or dubious but exciting and encouraging. This sensation may resemble the excitement before a long trip or a new adventure. It is not necessarily a sensation that something wrong could happen, but excitement for the new and the uncertainty it brings.

What you fear the most is nowhere close to what could happen and the list of things that can go wrong. You have to go deeper and find the root of that sensation. For example, you are not necessarily afraid of losing your job, going back and living with your parents and harming your credit score. The fear behind the event is more related to overthinking judgments you or the people would make, such as failure, guilt, resentment, and regret.

Overthinking what will happen is useless, a waste of energy and inner resources. And in general, all the excuses to procrastinate, like fear, come from the same source, the ego that sometimes also wants to sabotage you. And to move forward and take the leap of faith, you must understand and face that source.

However, don't confuse overthinking with thinking about what to do and planning your life, as we did in the previous chapter. What we did previously was putting dreams and desires into a map of possible execution to start acting, which is very different from thinking about what will go wrong.

When I decided to quit my job the last time, I had a scenario in my head. However, everything I overthought, especially the catastrophes that would happen, never really happened. The real problems in the Universe often come from what you never think of and manifest in unexpected ways. In my case, the situations I thought were the easy ones became the most challenging, and my biggest fears were the blessings in my path.

In the case of my clients, it is no different. The Universe normally is in charge of showing the path— the one of learning and expansion. Most of the negativity they bring from overthinking, and the external world vanishes. Opportunities start flowing only after a few weeks of working with me and starting to do the inner work. Some don't even finish the programs because the Universe gives them answers when they feel ready. They find big clients; they are offered the job opportunity they have been waiting for months or receive employment termination agreements that allow them to start their own business. But remember, tunning with the message of the Universe is a daily practice to know yourself better and to be in the present moment more often.

If you stay where you are without taking real action and keep complaining about all the things you don't like, we certainly know what will happen—you will be in the same situation in one, five, or ten years. We both know, you and me, why you are deciding to stay in an unsatisfying and frustrating place. However, there will always be "excitement" when making life-changing decisions, and you will never be sure what will happen. But don't let that sensation prevent you from being courageous and moving forward with your life's plan.

Before moving forward with the book and your decisions, I recommend you reconsider your fears by revising chapter four and connecting with the escapisms. You can make a new list of your fears with the understanding you acquired in the previous chapters. Then, remind yourself that whatever you are afraid of will never happen. The only certainty you have today is that you want to change your situation, and that will only happen if you allow yourself to listen to your soul and the signs universe. Finally, find your tones of truth again, define your new affirmations and change your thoughts and

Dealing with Family and Friends

There are no rules on how you face your family, friends, and people affected by your decisions. Some people trust their relatives, friends, or spouse when deciding on a big life change. They won't move a finger before they know how the other person feels about a decision. And if this is you, you can keep using the same strategies you used before, but always be careful when listening to advice and other opinions.

Every person you ask for an opinion or advice will speak from their fears, experience and limiting beliefs. And even when it is fine to sit down and comment to family and family about what you want to do, it is also a careful decision to specify who you want to listen to. Not everyone is always a good advisor.

Of course, I'm not telling you not to share what you want to do next with your family, especially your immediate family and spouse. They will, at some point, become active decision-makers, and a parallel plan will need to be completed for each one of the members of your immediate family. For example, you will need your spouse's support to move to another city, quit your job or make a significant investment. It is imperative to be aligned with them.

When I was deciding to leave my job at the firm before I moved to France, I received comments such as, "You are not 20 years old anymore, you should reconsider quitting and stay where you are, you are doing great," "You don't have enough money to pay for a master's in another country," "You are throwing seven years of work out of the window, you are making a wrong decision." They might have been right but were only right according to their egos.

My clients also receive the same kind of comments, especially when the decision is related to quitting their jobs or starting a new business—"what are you going to do for a living?" "you are crazy! How are you quitting the job you have been working on for the last 20 years?" "what? Nobody pays for that kind of service," "starting a new business today is impossible; you need to invest tons of money to be discovered on the Internet," "Who are you to start being a consultant or a coach? Nobody knows you," "what are your credentials to write a book or start a blog."

And when you start sharing your decisions, you will also find the same phrases from the people around you; people who don't understand you and probably will never understand you. However, these comments are not only fine, but they are also necessary. As you are doing real work to understand the root of your fears and to start understanding your place in the Universe, these comments about your life changes can bring new nuances and perspectives about your feelings. If, for example, you feel offended, insecure, or angry after a question or an opinion about your decision, understand the trigger to identify what needs some alignment. You do not necessarily adjust your plans; instead, you need to change the programs, the fears, the ideas, or the limiting beliefs.

When sharing your plans with others, please remember not to expect others to get close to the understanding of your life—not even the people closest to you. Not only our human condition is full of insecurities, but your goals and concept of success differ from the rest. You can definitively hear their opinions about your life and even thank them for their advice. They probably believe they know better than you and for sure want you to be happy; but happy according to their idea of happiness and not yours. Don't let discouraging comments affect your soul and your heart. Your dreams shouldn't collapse because someone has a different mindset, background, ambition, and points of view.

If you are strong and confident enough not to be affected by what others comment, it's your choice to decide whether you want to share your plans. But if you tend to be affected by comments and opinions, don't do it. In this case, and if you have identified negative, pessimistic individuals who tend to be the victims of the world and who are not your immediate family, don't share anything with them. Please keep it for yourself until you know where to go and when you have already started the path. You don't need those emotions at this moment in your life.

If, on the contrary, you have identified friends and family members who have been through similar situations and who have a very optimistic and confident perspective, call them to tell them your plans and ask for ideas. After talking to them, you will feel encouraged, lighter, and ready to move on. Especially if you have a business idea, don't keep anything for yourself. When you share ideas with these kinds of people, they will help you see outside of your box and introduce you to people that know someone who can help you or even partner with you. It is always better together, don't forget that.

When you reach a certain point of confidence, it does not matter who you talk with or share with. You will feel so sure of what you are doing; you are so aligned with what you want that nothing and no one can stop you. This courage is the point of no turning back; this is when you know you are ready, going on the right path, and unstoppable.

Planning with Your Immediate Family

When your decision affects others, implementing the *Job Decision Model* may be the time to involve them in the conversation and facilitate it. Telling your family that you have a big change in your life needs to come from the bottom of the heart, love and understanding. Be honest, be sincere, and don't keep anything for yourself. Nothing is wrong when you share from your heart and soul, even when the other person is not ready to accept it. Be patient with their lack of understanding; they also have that inner voice that is hard to control, telling them everything will be wrong. However, don't try to create any expectations about their reaction; you don't know exactly how they will react. Decisive determinations may trigger parts of their psyche that you have never known. Additionally, this book proposes a world's view so different from the status quo that it may also be bizarre for the previous version of yourself.

When making a critical decision with a family member, I recommend that each immediate family member reads the book. It may help them to understand better your point of view. If it is not possible, they should also complete the *Job Decision Model* sheet. Then you can share the result and identify where they converge and are unaligned. There is little to discuss when goals, passions and values are similar. However, it is important to discern together and discuss with understanding when there are differences.

We all have doubts, don't make the mistake of thinking that you know everything; because there are always different sides to the story, so listen to the ones you love. However, when it comes to your feelings, learn to set some boundaries because you are the only expert in the world. But overall, never let the opinions of others make you stop trusting yourself and your intuition

Be ready for everything, not by thinking about everything that will go wrong, but by expecting the unexpected. When big changes happen, the space between people and their energy levels also changes. If you feel that your loved ones are turning away and not really on the same page as you are, please don't freak out; it's normal. These reactions probably happen because they have never encountered that version of yourself, who, for the first time, is listening to yourself and not society's script. Opposite reactions may happen because you are ready to move on, while others don't imagine leaving their comfort zone just yet. However, disagreement doesn't mean you must divorce or end your relationships with those you love. Instead, it means that your path of expansion needs a few more challenges, that you must prove to the Universe that you are strong with your decision and that you need to open your heart as much as possible to understand others' points of view, even when it is judgment, criticism, jealousy and anger.

When fear is bigger than love, things tend to fall apart, and they will fall apart if you continue to live by the rules of your lowest frequencies. The probability of disappointment and regret is always there, and Mr. Ego is the first to welcome that state of mind. On the contrary, finding consensus is always possible when love is bigger than fear. Communication, understanding, and support will always be there. Additionally, when we trust and love ourselves, the Universe will eventually show the path, probably not in the form you expect or when you want, but if you are attentive to the signs, you will find it.

You are on Your Own. Trust the Universe

The following may sound tough, but you are the only person you have in your life. You are alone with whatever the Universe wants to provide and all the love you have for yourself and others. When you understand this as the truth, you liberate the unnecessary tension coming from the expectations of others. And instead, you start redirecting that energy to encourage yourself to do all necessary for your dreams and personal growth.

The day you understand this, everything changes because you stop being the victim of the circumstances and the people in your life. Instead, you start connecting with the energies of your inner sovereign and warrior to define where you want to go and how you will. The understanding that you are alone, from a space of love and connection with yourself and life itself, will switch your life from hell to heaven in seconds. It feels like an inner change of 180 degrees.

However, this reflection doesn't mean we are unsocial beings and don't need others to be complete, happy, and at peace; this means that life is about reaching your goals and knowing that no one else will do it for you. For example, no one is going to quit for you, no one is going to negotiate the new business you want to open, nobody will lose the weight you want, and nobody will write the book you want to write. Moreover, you are the only one who can work on your feelings, inner programs and how you are embracing your life.

Nobody except you can know your genuine fears, dreams, and values, and no one but you can understand the importance of your purpose. Nobody has been in your shoes and will ever be to understand all the nuances of your journey. Therefore, it's almost impossible for others to understand the path of your soul and all the little doors of consciousness in your mind. Imagine, if it is hard for us to be certain of our passions and purpose, how are you expecting others to get you?

We all have different stories to tell. Some people will be steadily growing in their lives and their careers, and little by little, building the future and the goals they want. Others make huge steps, and from nowhere, they are on the other side of the equation. Others need to fall, not only once but three or four times because they need to re-accommodate many pieces of their world to continue. Always remember, whenever you think you are falling without a parachute, it's exactly the opportunity you are looking for to grow spiritually and prepare yourself for the future. Don't waste those opportunities; embrace them as the most valuable teachers you'd ever have. Learn to love what is happening to you, even the impermanent discomfort. You will be a better person tomorrow, not only for others but better person for yourself.

The Universe loves you, and your soul knows it. You have had a magnificent life, and it will only get better. Even when you feel you are falling and alone in the race to find your purpose and realize your dreams, the Universe will unexpectedly provide all the necessary tools and resources. So, pay attention to take advantage of what you are receiving, and stop expecting specific people to do things or for certain things to happen.

You don't exactly know which part of the path to reach your dreams you are today. You may be falling or climbing a very difficult mountain. However, please do not pay attention to that because the map constantly moves as the Universe unfolds. Better focus on the compass and ensure you are not losing track of your purpose and values, and enjoy the ride. You will always find lakes, trees, and a refreshing breeze to take a break. You can always get rid of things you don't need anymore to travel lighter. Walk confidently, knowing that life will give you whatever you need even when it may get tiering and encouraging sometimes. As you keep working on maintaining your energies high, expanding your consciousness, and pursuing your goals, the Universe will answer the calls of your soul and your real self

Fixing Your Life in One Day

When facing a hard decision, your ego and mind start playing with you. The saboteur instinct of Mr. ego is always thinking about time, overthinking what will happen tomorrow, in a month, or a year. This behavior will overwhelm you and makes you believe you cannot take care of all the commitments and situations to come. However, you better not play that game when making a radical change in your life. It is like thinking that you need to know the phone number to take a taxi to the airport when going on vacation the next summer. You only need that information once you are with your luggage at the door, and not before. Start by thinking first about where you want to go and which transportation you would prefer to get there, instead of getting worried because you need the taxis' company number. You don't need to plan your vacation in one day, as well as you cannot fix your entire life.

If you need to sell your house, you won't sell it tomorrow; there is a long process. If you need to write a resignation letter, you can write it five minutes before the appointment. If you need to make a financial plan, you will do it when you have time on Sunday morning, don't think about it today. If you need to learn a new skill, it will take little steps performed every day. Face life today and whatever it brings with love and optimism, but remember, from the *Job Decision Model,* the true priorities you should be working on every day.

I recommend you print your list of goals and stick it on your fridge, bathroom mirror, or nightstand, at least for a while. Then, continuously remind yourself you will have the life you dream of by working on those activities. You may be weeks away from something unexpectedly good and changing your life.

Just Do It

We live in one of the most amazing moments of our civilization. As human beings, we can do things that our ancestors never imagined. We have discovered a lot about how our bodies and our brains work. We have amazing theories about how the Universe was made and why galaxies and planets move as they do. We know what is happening on the other side of the world in seconds and can be on different continents in just a few hours. But despite all this, the collective consciousness of our civilization was not ready yet to appreciate all the magnificence of the human experience. So rather than enjoying it, we are stressed trying to be productive and get more stuff, and overwhelmed by infinite information blowing into our minds every second, telling us how we should live our lives, what a perfect life looks like, and how imperfect we all are.

We have fed our negative ego to the point that we have forgotten our human nature and don't even care about it. We don't understand who we are, why we feel what we feel, and where we are going. We are trying to feed our ego with anything we can—more things and more possessions—without even understanding why we need all of that. We are doing it just for the sake of doing it, just because we have been told to do so by the "invisible hand" of our society.

It is time to make a hard stop in our lives, not only as individuals but as human beings in general and ask ourselves what we need to do at this moment, in this form, in this place to have better lives, to build a better future. You can start with purpose and the passions already inside you and work towards your goals now—not tomorrow, not in a year when you have a better job. Life is today, and you have today only; stop wasting your minutes, hours, and weeks listening to what you are not according to society.

If you read this book consciously, you now have the tools to feel more confident and decide to choose your love side, be fearless, and trust yourself, no matter what you decide forward. Stay tuned with your intuition; never stop working on that. Listen to yourself continuously and decide to stop suffering for the inventions of your mind — the situations you don't know exist, that never happened, and probably never will.

Take advantage of everything the world has today—information, technology, the Internet, and globalization, not to complain, criticize, or feed your insecurities, but to look for new ideas, ways of living, and opportunities. Use technology to feed your soul with joy, to change your world and the world of the ones you love. A joyful life is one of the best legacies we can leave to ourselves and the world.

Uncover your soul, rediscover who you are, and find the child you have inside; he/she has never left you. Come back to the awareness of the now without worrying about what will happen tomorrow. Tomorrow is not here yet, and in fact, tomorrow will never be here, you are always in the eternal now. We don't know how life will unfold, but we always expect the best of the Universe without expecting anything for anybody.

You are on your own, the creator, and ultimately the person responsible for your happiness. How you embrace life is the only thing you can control, through your thoughts, words, what you decide to watch and eat, your awareness, and your consciousness. Do not waste those superpowers; use them and let your ego sleep more often. Life is beautiful when it is not around.

Dream, and dream beautifully. Never stop dreaming. Ten-year-olds and 20-year-olds are not the only ones with the right to dream. We are still here in this space-time, and dreaming is free. Dream the plan of your life, and be certain you will have everything you know you deserve. Dream about what you want for the planet and the people who will inhabit it in 1,000 years so you can start making that happen; your legacy will be on this earth forever because death is never the end of who you are.

Love yourself as the biggest treasure you will ever have. You are the creator, the Universe, the consciousness that perceives everything around you, and the spirit that needs to move to a higher energy level. So, stop judging yourself; there is nothing wrong. Everything is what it has to be, even what you perceive as bad today. Thousands of hundreds of things are happening during billions of years of evolution, and those things are not happening to you; they are happening for you to witness.

Be authentic, be the sole version of yourself. Integrity is a value we forgot when we changed the priorities of our lives. Live your values, never forget about them, and if you need to accommodate them to come closer to your soul, do it, but remember to live your values every second. Stop pretending to be someone you are not because you want to fit in with your family, friend or the workplace. Denying your truth causes a lot of unconscious pain. Nothing that happens in your life is a failure or anything to feel shame about. It's your life and will only belong to you regardless of what others think of you; the only person's actions you should be concerned about are yours. What others do or think of you is their problem; it is their way of seeing life and their ego making comparisons to feed them with more insecurities.

When you are on the side of love, the fearless side, and living a life without judgment, you will attract people with the same energy levels. So, if you feel rejection when living in with more joy and peace, you are vibrating in different frequencies. The important thing, in this case, is to be aware and not let yourself fall back to negative energy again. Accept all the changes to come, even when they generate discomfort. You know now that you can transform that discomfort into strength to keep fighting for what you desire.

Do not sabotage yourself anymore. Whatever you always wanted to do, start it now. Stop feeding yourself with excuses and fear. Stop filling the to-do list with more things to do but never start. What you can do now, please do it now. If you want to open a restaurant, look for space to rent today. If you want to start painting again, buy the oils now; order online, and they will arrive in a few days. If you want to lose weight, discard all processed food in your cabinets and from your fridge. If you want to change the world, start from within by raising your consciousness and how you see the Universe. If you want a new job, discover why you need that change and re-establish what you want.

You are a superhero or a goddess; find someone to help you to upgrade your superpowers; whatever the price may be, it's nothing compared to the benefit of achieving your dreams and finding joy and peace in your life. A new car, a bigger house, the latest iPhone, a new certification, or a new master's won't change your life. Instead, find a coach if you need guidance; there are tons of us out there waiting to serve, help, make a change, fulfill our purpose, to live our passion. Start investing in your soul; it is never, never, never too late.

Acknowledgments

I'm grateful for everything that has happened in my life: the place I was born, the parents I have, my sister, the school I studied at, and the jobs that I've had—without any of each of those experiences, none of these words would have been possible.

Thanks to my mom, father, and sister, who were there wishing the best for me even when thinking I was losing my mind.

I also feel very grateful because the universe conspired so I could make this book a reality.

Thanks to the Author Incubator team and Angela E. Laurina for creating this magnificent program to improve this world.

Thanks to my husband Steve for his support and his trust in my work

Thanks to my coaches and mentors, Andres Rozo Echeverry and Jeremy Lasman, their way of looking at the world finally made me understand I belonged to something bigger.

Thanks to Carolina Palacio and Mauricio Sanchez for their amazing cover design—what would I do without your creativity?

Thanks to the launching team for committing to be part of this journey without hesitation and with all their hearts.

Thanks to the people who allowed me to be their coach. I am honored to be part of your lives.

Thanks to the consultants, professionals and friends who stepped aside from their daily lives and allowed me to interview them.

About the Author

Juliana Tabares is a business consultant and executive coach with over 15 years of experience working with multinational corporations. Throughout her consulting career, Juliana has focused on helping organizations improve their internal processes to become more efficient while complying with regulations. She has worked in several countries and interacted with people from more than 30 nationalities, gaining a deep understanding of the global business landscape and global cultural differences.

However, Juliana always felt like something was missing from her corporate work. She realized that organizations' goals often contradicted human beings' collective purposes and goals, prompting her to explore how to harmonize her job and her purpose in life. In 2010, she started using coaching tools to find her direct purpose in life.

In 2017, Juliana's search for purpose led her to delve deeper into spirituality, where she discovered that personal growth is the most important work we can do in our lives. This realization, combined with her love for science, religion, and Buddhism, motivated her to step away from the business world and write a book to empower her fellow coworkers.

Originally from Colombia, Juliana has lived and worked in France and the United States. She holds an engineering background and an Executive Master's in Business Administration. Today, Juliana is a full-time coach and independent consultant, dedicated to her clients and researching and developing new tools for professionals and leaders to discover their purpose and achieve their goals for themselves and their organizations.

Thank You

Thank you for investing time in your life and your personal growth, nothing makes me happier than this. Your transformation is the real reason I wrote this book.

Please keep in touch and don't hesitate if you want to have a call, I know what it feels like to be overwhelmed and confused when making an important decision in your life. You only need to schedule a call on my webpage: https://onelifetobeyou.com/

You can also follow my follow me on LinkedIn: https://www.linkedin.com/in/juliana-tabares/

Don't forget to review the book on Amazon:
- https://www.amazon.com/dp/B07FFF66WK/ (Digital)
- https://www.amazon.com/dp/1731485980 (PaperBack)

www.ingramcontent.com/pod-product-compliance
Lightning Source LLC
Chambersburg PA
CBHW031534210526
45464CB00013B/49